WHAT IS EDUCATION?

WHAT IS EDUCATION?

Ernest Carroll Moore

General Books

A General Books LLC Publication.

CONTENTS

1

SECTION 1

PREFACE

This volume owes its inception to my efforts to teach college students and teachers how to study. As I have attempted year after year to discuss with my classes the ways and means of performing the student's work, the conviction has grown upon me that one of the greatest needs both of teachers and of students at present is an elementary knowledge of the philosophy of education. Two conclusions have shaped themselves from this conviction, which stand out above all the rest. The first is that education is one and the same process in all grades of schools, and that the activities which we learn to perform with the help and guidance of teachers are the very activities which we shall have to continue to perform until we die. The second is that the confusion as to the nature of their undertaking, which hangs like a thick cloud about the efforts of teachers and students, cannot be dissipated save by an attempt to answer the question, What is knowledge ? The theory of knowledge has long been the battle ground of contending philosophical armies. It was the vital question of the great apostles of education, Socrates and Plato, before it became the private property of highly technical philosophical schools. It must once more, I believe, become one of the chief concerns of educators.

This book, therefore, is an attempt to discuss some of the fundamental presuppositions of education. It is a series of essays, somewhat closely related, upon a few of the subjects which I believe that we who follow the profession of teaching must perpetually keep turning over in our minds in order that clear ideas upon them may shape and control our work.

I have attempted not only to set forth my own views upon these problems, but, when opportunity offered, to re- enforce them by the statements of other men. " Have you ever observed that we pay more attention to a wise passage when it is quoted than when we read it in the original author ?" writes Hamerton. I have felt that I had a duty to attempt to secure for some wise passages which bear very immediately upon the theory of education as much attention as I can.

The notions of education which I have attempted to outline I have learned chiefly from Socrates and Plato. My indebtedness to two living teachers, Professor John Dewey and Professor Frank McMurry, I gratefully acknowledge; it will be apparent to everyone who may do me the honor to turn the leaves of this book.

ERNEST C. MOORE

Cambridge, Massachusetts

Hamlet. . . . Will you play upon this pipe ?

Guildenslern. My lord, I cannot.

Hamlet. I pray you.

Guildenstern. Believe me, I cannot.

Hamlet. I do beseech you.

Guildenstern. I know no touch of it, my lord.

Hamlet. It is as easy as lying : govern these ventages with your fingers and thumb, give it breath with your mouth, and it will discourse most eloquent music. Look you, these are the stops.

Guildenstern. But these cannot I command to any utterance of harmony ; I have not the skill.

Hamlet. Why, look you now, how unworthy a thing you make of me. You would play upon me ; you would seem to know my stops; you would pluck out the heart of my mystery ; you would sound me from my lowest note to the top of my compass; and there is much music, excellent voice, in this little organ; yet cannot you make it speak. 'Sblood! do you think I am easier to be played on than a pipe ? Call me what instrument you will, though you can fret me, you cannot play upon me. | Shakespeare, *Hamlet,* III, ii

" All architecture," said Whitman, " is what you do to it when you look upon it ... all music is what awakes from you when you are reminded by the instruments." | Quoted in the article, " Railway Junctions " in *The Unpopular Review,* Vol. II, No. 3

Beloved Pan, and all ye other gods who haunt this place; give me beauty in the inward soul; and may the outward and inward man be at one.| Plato, Phajdrus, 279

For, behold, the kingdom of God is within you.| Luke xvii, 21

Agesilaus was once asked what he thought most proper for boys to learn. What they ought to do when men, was the reply. | Montaigne

WHAT IS EDUCATION?

CHAPTER I

WHAT IS EDUCATION?

Years ago, while a student in New York City, I
attended a meeting of the Graduate Club of Columbia, which was addressed by some three or four of the leading professors of the University upon the subject, " How I came to choose the work which I am now doing." I remember that on that occasion Professor Brander Matthews told us how, as a student living in a garret in Paris, he made the acquaintance of the French drama; and Professor Franklin Giddings, how he came to devote his life to sociology; and that Professor, now President, Nicholas Murray Butler gave an account somewhat like this, of how he came to study education. He said: " I was a junior in Columbia College when one day, as I was passing President Barnard's door, he called me into his office and said, ' Butler, what do you mean to do when you get out of college ?' I replied: ' Mr. President, I have not decided, but I shall probably study law.' Then President Barnard
replied: ' Butler, do not do it. There are plenty of lawyers already. Study education. In this country it is an unbroken field. There is no subject which so much merits study or which will yield larger return in point of opportunities for service to him who makes himself an authority in it than this subject of education.' I replied, in a more or less vague way, that I did not know what he meant by education in that sense. He replied by giving me Ludwig Wiese's ' German Letters on English Education,' and asked me to read it, and after I had read it to come back and talk it over with him. I did read this book and became greatly interested in the whole field of reflection and study which it opened up. As a result, I read under President Barnard's guidance, during my next summer holiday, Karl von Raumer's ' Geschichte der Padagogik.' He pointed out that I must be sure to study philosophy in order to have a basis upon which to build any genuine knowledge of educational theory and practice. With this, I was launched on what proved to be my professional career."

The advice which President Barnard gave is not often given by university men to their students, yet his reasons for giving it are as sound to-day as when he uttered them. There is no subject which so much deserves study, or which offers larger opportunities for service to mankind than this.

Education is one of the major concerns of the race. The chiefs of the philosophers have regarded it as the one thing needful for the perfecting of states and the improving of lives. Civilized nations have taken its claims so seriously that giving instruction and attending upon instruction is now the occupation in which the largest numbers of their people are engaged. What was formerly the privilege of the few is now compulsory for all. The very magnitude of this undertaking puts it above the plane of indifference. The seriousness of the issues involved is such as to give the most unimaginative person who for a moment contemplates them a sense of responsibility almost too great for mortals to bear. Other occupations work with things or with human interests taken singly. This occupation assumes a guardianship over the generations which affects all that they do. The directors of schools, the makers of courses of study, and the teachers of the young are engaged in " choosing experiences for people," not for a day or an hour but for life. The study of education is the effort to put intelligence into that high task. " Nothing is worth doing, which is not worth thinking about." The world, even the educated world, is quick to see that education is worth doing, but slow to admit that it is worth thinking about. Gradually it is being won over from its reliance upon the customary and the traditional, andhesitatingly it begins to examine the life which it prescribes for the young. The first fruits of intelligence applied to education are better laws and administrative devices. These produce a better teaching personnel. Yet this is but a beginning of reforms. Those who teach must think about the experiences which they choose for those who are taught.

One of the earliest books written in this country upon the work of the teacher begins with the question, " Why is it that there is such a ' singular contrariety of opinion in regard to the pleasantness of the business of teaching ?' " Some teachers regard their daily task as intolerable drudgery, others never cease to think and to talk of " their delightful labors." The answer is that " every mind is so constituted as to take a positive pleasure in the exercise of ingenuity, in adapting means to an end, and in watching their operation." 1 Those who do this find pleasure in their work, those who do not, regard it as drudgery. This continuous adapting of means to ends is not only the sole expedient for vitalizing the teacher, it is the sole method of vitalizing the school and of vitalizing education itself. This is the thinking which is enjoined upon all who work at anything which is worth doing. Theory and practice must go hand in hand, for theory is nothing but thinking about practice, andthe practice which is worth while must be thought about, that is, must grow out of theory. The notion that theory and practice should work together in education is older even than Socrates, for the first of the culture teachers of the Greeks, the greafl Protagoras, left the world these two conclusions from his reflection upon education: the first, " teaching requires natural disposition and exercise, and must be begun in youth "; the second, " neither theory without practice nor practice without theory i avails at all." 1

1 Jacob Abbott, The Teacher. Boston, 1834. 1 Gomperz, Greek Thinkers, 1-p. 441.

Some uses of theory. Without theory, practice must be a blind doing of what somebody else | tradition, authority, or accident | has directed. Rational purpose is lacking, there is no selecting of aims, no turning over of plans to decide which is best, and little checking up to find out the real worth of what has been accomplished. The individual situation is slighted. The authorities do the thinking, if indeed any is done. Other members of the undertaking are only hands to carry out their orders. " Tell us exactly what should be done in a high school, and we will go and do it," say our students sometimes to us. The teacher can no more maintain himself on such a basis than the physician can. The principles of medicine are not rule-of- thumb recipes which tell him exactly what to do inevery given case. They are laws and rules which he must use to interpret his patients' needs. No one can fit the rules to the given case who does not know them and their advisory character. They are not guide-board directions; instead they call for application, since they always take the hypothetical form: if, in your practice, you find these conditions, it is best to proceed thus or thus. To attempt to work out the details of the procedure of education, apart from its concrete situations, results only in mechanizing instruction.

The kind of practice which has value. Teachers when seeking a situation, frequently offer their long experience as an inducement to prospective employers to engage them. But it is not quantity of practice but quality of practice which determines expertness.

Practice which has not led to reflection or been thought about atrophies intelligence. The merest beginner who brings his mind to his work is incalculably superior to such a routine instructor. A wholesome doubt as to the sufficiency of what we are doing makes improvement possible. The race has not yet found out how to educate its children, though it has been trying for many years. Let us have theories, plenty of theories, the more the better, since we can hardly have too many minds at work upon this most difficult and urgent of problems. None but the mind saturatedwith knowledge and well stocked with visions of the possibilities of education can detect the shortcomings of its procedure. None but the theorist can discriminate its strength from its weakness, or actually see what is being done. None but the theorist can introduce experiments, devise standards, suggest alternatives, or predict the probable outcome of a given course of action. "It is highly probable," writes Professor Baldwin, " that two in every three children are more or less damaged or hindered in their mental and moral development in the school; but," he adds, " I am not at all sure that they would fare any better if they stayed at home! " There are plenty of problems to be solved.

The wisely practical educator and the practical theorist are the only persons who can solve them; the mere theorist, or the mere taker of orders, is as useless in education as he is everywhere else.

Three grades of knowledge. There are three grades of knowledge which one may have of any given subject matter. They are usually distinguished as ordinary, or common-sense, knowledge, scientific knowledge, and philosophic knowledge. Each of these grades of knowledge is due to a grouping, or classification, of experiences, and in each of them we take a present or a past experience as the sign of a future one which we seek to bring into being or to escape from. Thesethree grades of knowledge deal with the same phenomena, but from different standpoints. They are throughout one in kind. Difference of subject matter to which they apply is not the mark which distinguishes them. It is commonly believed that ordinary knowledge does not enable one to predict, whereas scientific knowledge does. Yet every boy who drops a stone into the water knows beforehand that it will sink, as certainly as the scientist does. And every time one strikes a match, discharges a gun, or puts fire beneath water, seeds into the ground, or food on the table, he does so because he predicts that certain results will happen. Human action of the most ordinary kind is based upon this power to predict. Wherein, then, does the superiority of scientific knowledge to common- sense knowledge lie ? The boy cannot tell how fast the stone will fall. The scientist can. The man who discharges the gun cannot follow the series of changes which drive the bullet forward, or trace its course, or calculate the force of its impact. Science consists in the minuter examination of experience. It seeks quantitative precision, where common sense reckons with a vague more-or-less. It coordinates remote happenings and traces relations among them which common sense had not suspected, as between the fall of an apple and the movement of a world, the death of a man fromyellow fever and the prevalence of a certain insect, etc. Common-sense knowledge tends to be personal. Its facts are conceived in relation to a self, while science strives to be impersonal and to relate its facts to the body of facts which surround them. In order to trace relations between wide ranges of facts, science disengages the identities, which it traces, from the particularities which attend them, and states its results as abstract laws and systems of laws. Rub a board with a bit of sandpaper, or a piece of brass with a rag. The board or the piece of brass becomes hot. The common-sense fact is that this board, when rubbed, became hot. Science omits the details of the experience and fixes its attention upon the relations. " Friction produces heat " is the fact which it gathers.

" If you want to know anything about education in the United States, ask the first man you meet on the street " is the advice which Superintendent McClymonds gave to Professor John Adams when he visited America. There is, however, a difference between common-sense knowledge of education and scientific knowledge of it, though the man in the street may not recognize it. There is a scientific knowledge of school legislation, of the way to build a schoolhouse, of school administration, of selecting the subjects for a course of study, and a scientific knowledge of children and of the procedure whichmust be employed in instructing them. This knowledge, though by no means as exact as it is certain to become, is very considerable in extent and significant in value. Though as yet it is only to a slight degree quantitative in character, it is nevertheless definitely scientific, in the same sense that comparative anatomy is scientific. School administration is a branch of government. It has been studied rather more intensively than most of the problems of government. Comparative methods have been employed, and conclusions of great directive value have been reached. It does not detract in the slightest degree from the worth and validity of these systematized conclusions that they are not commonly consulted when plans for administering school systems are being devised, just as it does not detract from the reality of a science of medicine for one who is sick to consult a quack rather than a scientific physician. The fact remains that in both cases minute and careful study has developed a body of knowledge more thoroughgoing and reliable than uncritical experience provides, which stands ready for use by anyone who will use it.

Genetic psychology likewise offers parents and teachers the rich results of its tireless researches into the nature and growth of the child. General psychology outlines the principles which governthe behavior of mind. Ethics, sociology, biology, and medicine contribute their quota of principles to be reduced to practice. The history of education outlines the experiments which the race has made in preparing the young for their life work, and the sufficiency or insufficiency of the social aims and methods which directed that preparation. The languages, literatures, and sciences which provide the subject matter of instruction have been reduced to teachable form. The comparative study of the provisions for education which progressive nations have made furnishes a systematized knowledge of educational practice throughout the civilized world.

Though education is among the last of human institutions to invoke the aid of scientific method, it will thus be seen that scientific method has entered it, and that no one engaged in it is limited to rule-of-thumb knowledge. There is a science of education whose rich resources are available to anyone who will use them.

Philosophic knowledge versus scientific knowledge. The science of education, like every other science, deals only with the coexistences and sequences of its particular field of facts. It is one among many sciences, each of which studies the world from its own standpoint. As yet it has made only a beginning, but even if it succeeds in tilling its field, like the other sciences it will possess only afragment of knowledge. Ask the astronomer what the universe is, and he will describe it in terms of astronomy. Ask the geologist, and he will answer in terms of geology. Ask the student of politics, and he will describe it in terms of organizations of government. And ask the educator, and he will answer in terms of schools and teaching. Is there no form of knowledge which relates all these different sciences together, which can answer such a question in terms common to them all I no science of things in general which can give us a picture of the universe as it is ? Education must become one of the sciences. Is there no science of sciences to unify its work with theirs, to correlate its truths with the whole body of truth? That function belongs to philosophy. Its work begins where science leaves off. It concerns itself with a critical examination of the hypotheses and assumptions which the sciences make in order to solve their problems. It examines their foundation principles, criticizes their concepts, and pieces together their systematizations. It is an unusually persistent effort to think matters down to their roots and out to their conclusions. While, in its criticism of the categories and systematization of the results of other forms of knowledge, it does not add to the facts which the sciences amass, it does endeavor to determine their meaning, and the knowledge whichit supplies is knowledge rendered more exact and usable through consistency of interpretation.

One frequently hears the statement that philosophy is of little worth. Quite recently it has been pointed out that, since it is theoretical, the practical business man has no need for it I unless he is a very practical man. The strangest thing about it is that no one can get along without it. As soon as we begin to think at all, each one of us sets about making a philosophy for himself, and never leaves off the work of constructing it until he dies. The difference between a common-sense philosophy and a critical and systematic one is somewhat analogous to the difference between common-sense knowledge and scientific knowledge; that is, the latter is more thorough than the former, is made more carefully, its parts articulate better, it gives us a larger world which has more depth and steadfastness in it.

Whether one's philosophy is homemade or academically constructed, we must agree with Mr. Chesterton that the view of the universe which he keeps is the most practical and important thing about him. " We think that for a landlady considering a lodger it is important to know his income, but still more important to know his philosophy. We think that for a general about to fight an enemy, it is important to know the enemy'snumbers, but still more important to know the enemy's philosophy. We think the question is not whether the theory of the cosmos affects matters, but whether in the long run anything else affects them." 1 And to us it seems that by far the most important thing about a teacher is the kind of philosophy of education which he carries about with him. How one couples up his notions of education with the scheme of things seems to us to be the most illuminating item that can be known about him. Indeed, so thoroughly do basic conceptions determine conduct that if he will tell us definitely and clearly what he thinks education is, we, on our part, will undertake to tell what methods he uses and what success attends his work. Can a teacher who has a wrong notion of what education is be a good teacher? Not if teaching is a conscious process. Can a teacher who has worked out a sound philosophy of education be a poor teacher? Not if ideas shape and determine practice. On the other hand, it seems to us that the teacher who lacks a sound philosophy of education is like a ship without a compass; he may pursue any course, or go anywhere, for he has no means of determining where he is or in what direction he is moving. What is education ? seems to us, therefore, to be the most fundamental of all the questions which

1 G. K. Chesterton, Heretics.

condition the teacher's work. It cannot be answered dogmatically. A merely verbal reply to it, committed for purposes of ready reference, will not do. Out of the fullness of his own inner conviction each one must answer it in terms of his philosophy of life, and, like the other features of our philosophy of life, it is one of the fundamental problems which we should carry about with us and be constantly turning over in mind in an unceasing effort to allow no opportunity of revising our knowledge of it to escape us. There is no other way to work out a philosophy of education.

Two typical definitions of education. There are a great many definitions which profess to tell us what education is. Let us consider two of them which are somewhat typical. The first is that education is the imparting of knowledge. While education undoubtedly has something to do with knowledge, it is hardly its function to impart it. It is not good form to say, " I learned him geometry or reading." The verb *to learn* will not bear that meaning. I may teach him geometry or reading, but he must do his learning of them for himself. Is it not just as wrong to use the verb *teach* in the sense in which we are forbidden to use the verb *learn,* and to say, " I taught him geometry or reading," meaning by that, " I imparted them to him " ? I may keep a confectioner's shop and hand out candyto you when you come to buy, or a coal yard and shovel coal into your cellar when you give me an order, but I cannot hand out knowledge or shovel it into the minds of students, no matter how willing they may be to get it in that fashion. Knowledge is not that sort of thing, and whatever schools may be, they are not knowledge shops.

There is another sort of definition of education which, in attempting to escape the crudities of the one just given, involves itself in an even greater absurdity. The upholders of this view reason somewhat like this: "Minds are very imperfect things at birth. If left to themselves, they grow up quite incomplete. It is the business of education to complete them. Its object is not to supply knowledge to them, for that indeed it cannot do, but it must discipline them, exercise them, build them up, draw them out, and form them. A mind which has not been drawn out will never come out of itself. No one should think of using so crude and dull an instrument as mind is before it is sharpened. It is the business of education to perfect the mind."

I am profoundly convinced that, whatever else the teacher must do, he is never called upon to get inside the mind and do any burnishing or repair work there. We use a figure of speech when we talk of the gardener causing the plant to grow, and surely we use a figure of speech, and a verymisleading one, when we speak of education as the process of molding, sharpening, forming, or perfecting minds. Much as it may contribute to our pride to think of ourselves as performing such a service, the thing is inconceivable. We have no such creative power. In the Harvard Club in Boston there is one room set apart for the use of the graduates of the Medical School, and over the fireplace in that room there is an inscription, a motto, which states in a sentence the philosophy of the medical profession. It reads, " We dress the wound, God heals it." If a devoted student of education should attempt to construct a similar motto which would in like manner set forth the object of his profession, what form ought it to take ? This, I think: " We feed the mind, God makes it."

What is education ? When we teach we do not " learn " our students anything; they must do that for themselves. The notion that language conveys thought or vehicles thought is the root of the error that education exists to impart thought. And when we teach we do not make minds or strengthen minds or draw them out. The mistake of deriving the word *education* from the wrong Latin troot was, from the point of view of its consequences, one of the most serious mistakes that the race has yet made. What do we do? Let us see. When a feeble-minded child comes to school, the wiseteacher does not attempt to supply him with the regulation stock of knowledge, and she does not attempt to make his mind over. Neither of these things is possible. But there are certain things which even a feeble-minded child can learn to do that are socially useful and individually profitable. The wise teacher gives him a chance to do these things; that is, to use his mind, not to exercise it merely, and not to take knowledge, but, by comprehending what he can comprehend, to make knowledge. The pathological case supplies the insight we require concerning the normal one. Education must everywhere proceed in the same fashion. From the standpoint of the learner, it is the process of using one's own mind in socially profitable ways in the making of knowledge. From the standpoint of the school, it is the process of providing the conditions which necessitate the child's using his own mind in socially profitable ways in the making of knowledge. The teacher cannot supply knowledge and cannot make mind; his function is to provide the environment I to direct the child to the facts and methods of handling them which have been found to be socially useful, and to leave the rest to him.

Three kinds of schools. There are three kinds of schools which grow out of these three conceptions of education. According to the first kind, the greatthing is knowledge. It is stored up in books, in courses of study, and in the minds of teachers and other learned folks. Schools exist to retail it to young people, to pass it on from the places where it is to the places where it is not. That it may be passed on easily, it must be prepared in little carefully molded cubes or accurately weighed doses. That is the work of textbook makers and of manufacturers of methods. Teaching, according to this view, consists in seeing to it that the learner takes the proper number of pellets of knowledge each day, and the object of the recitation is to find out whether or not he has done so. Since what he has taken is knowledge in its essential form, he must retain it in the form in which he took it. To see that he has done this and is continuing to do it, there must be periodical inspections of his stock of knowledge. These are called examinations. They occur at regular intervals, since the amassing of a fixed amount of knowledge and the retention of it in its original condition is thought to be necessary before one can safely amass further knowledge.

The object of education according to this view is knowledge. The business of teaching is to put it where it is not. Textbooks are to provide it. Recitations are to find out whether or not it has been taken. Memory must retain it, and examinations must be given to test the knowledge state ofpupils. Since knowledge is the one thing needful, the quantity of knowledge which can be compressed into the memory of a school child becomes a matter of vast importance. Courses of study are written chiefly, in many cases, to indicate the quantity which every good retailer of knowledge must succeed in lodging in the memory of each child. To cover the prescribed amount of work is the mark toward which the teacher is made to press and toward which she is usually, in such a system, overpressed. That the directing authorities may know that teacher and pupils are handling the required stint of knowledge, that teachers may know that pupils are stocking themselves with it and retaining it in undiminished state, that parents may know that their children are amassing the fixed heaps of prescribed facts, that the children themselves may know how much they know, great reliance is placed on examinations. They are given with great regularity. Their results are carefully tabulated. Children are weighed and measured by them, are encouraged or discouraged, are promoted or demoted by them. As soon as one is over, everybody settles down to prepare for the next one. This is called an examination system of schools.

It is conceivable that either a university or a kindergarten might be conducted in this way. Fortunately they are not, but elementary schools,secondary schools, and colleges, not a few, are. The method is of long standing. Dr. McLean, formerly the head of the Pacific Theological School, once told me how he was taught theology at Princeton fifty years ago. He said: " Each day the professor brought our meat into the classroom cut up into neatly prepared little cubes, all of the same size. He then proceeded to insert the proper number of these into the stomach of each one of us. Two days after he looked into our stomachs to see if we were retaining them in the exact form in which he had given them to us."

The second kind of school tends to regard knowledge as something common and unclean. It claims a loftier mission. It sets out to sharpen and perfect the mind by putting it to work not on matters that it will have to work on as long as its possessor lives, but on special teaching disciplines, valuable not because of the opportunities for knowledge- getting which they provide, but for the mental exercises which one can perform in pursuing them. What you manipulate, they say, does not count. That you manipulate is the great thing. The best mental exercises are those which have been used so long that a perfect technique of using them has been developed. There are certain studies which are made much of in this type of school because they train the students not in the *object* matterwith which they profess to deal but in ratiocination in general. They provide hard work and plenty of it. They demand exactness. They enable teachers to assign fixed lessons of graduated difficulty, to require a system of recitations and examinations which tell exactly whether the student is meeting the requirements of the assignment or no. It makes little difference that the student after six or seven years of such labor will seem to himself to have learned nothing. The fact is that his mind will be *a.* much more flexible and ready instrument because

rbf this gymnastic. These are the mind-training schools. They make use of all the machinery which the others employ except the important element of knowledge.

The third kind of school believes both in knowledge and in mental training, but it holds that they ,go together and cannot possibly be separated. It asserts that knowledge is inner conviction, organizing experience in terms of vital need, and that, while mind can be trained specifically to organize experiences, since different experiences call each for its appropriate form of reaction, mind cannot be trained in general to make

them. This school looks upon knowledge not as a fixed and immutable thing but as a useful tool which men have shaped to
' meet their needs in living. It is not at all finished or final. Men made it by thinking, and men willimprove it by thinking, and before anyone can use it, or any part of it, he must remake it through his own thinking for himself. What Moses thought or Plato thought or Euclid thought will never do me any good until I succeed in thinking it for myself The great thing then for this school is not knowledge, but learning to use one's own mind upon matters which men have found to be important by using their minds upon them. Textbooks are important because they suggest to us some things which the race has found it important for us to think about. Teachers are important because they stimulate us to think by surrounding us with problems and reasons for solving them and such help in going about the matter in profitable ways as we stand in need of. They help us to look at things and study things and talk about things and repeat things and memorize things which can best be thought about in these ways. And from tiine to time, to make both us and themselves better acquainted with the success which we are achieving in our thinking, they set specific pieces of work for us to perform and examine our performance of them with somewhat greater care than they can give to our day-by-day thinking. It is not the amount of ground which we cover or the number of courses which we " take " which decides whether or no we are getting an education, according to this
! conception. Education is determined by what the student does. A single subject which has been pursued in such a way that he has learned to stand on his own feet and use his own mind in the getting and solving of its problems provides a more real education than a whole college course in which one has merely endeavored to appropriate the thoughts of other men or tried to become a thinker without thinking about anything which seemed to require thought. The first kind of school seeks to put its students in possession of results without allowing them to go through the processes of getting them. The second kind of school seeks to develop processes apart from the context of reality which gives them meaning. Its instruction goes on in a vacuum. It produces "thoughtless thinkers " ; while the first kind does not set out to make thinkers at all, and is rarely disappointed by having them develop.

What can education do? No one of these kinds of schools exists in a pure state; as we know them, they are only tendencies. Usually a keen discriminator of educational practices | such as students themselves commonly are | finds all three kinds living under the same roof. Their presence makes for variety. Like certain religiously considerate communities of old, institutions of learning consciously practice the habit of erecting altars to allof them, because they are unwilling to take any chance of not worshiping the true God. This procedure' is rather harder upon the students than upon the teachers, for "free trade in learning," which is dear to teachers, involves much compulsory miseducation which is destructively costly to students.

If schools exist to feed the minds of students, and in the nature of the case they can do nothing else, they must regard their function as that of purveying the raw materials of knowledge. Bread and meat are not food until the individual who would get nourishment from them has himself reduced them to chyle. At that point they enter the blood and provide nourishment; that is, these raw materials must be digested before they become available. To *digest* means to " tear apart," or separate the nutritious part from the innutritious' part. When our private digestive laboratories have done this the human system, through its circulatory department, sets about reorganizing the chyle which it has prepared, by building human tissue out of it. In its main features the learning process is quite analogous. What is commonly called knowledge is only / the raw material of knowledge I merely the opportunity for the making of knowledge. Before it can be converted into vitalizing knowledge, it must be; mentally digested and reorganized into personal

feeling, conviction, and action. When we speak of knowledge as a something stored up in books or records ready to be drawn off by anyone who will but open them, we must remember, as Bacon has told us, that " words are generally framed and applied according to the conception of the vulgar, and draw lines of separation according to such differences as the vulgar can follow." Knowledge has no such existence. It is always personal, though not necessarily private. It resides nowhere but in the mind which organizes it. Between the raw materials of food and muscular fitness for work there goes a long process of organic construction. Between the raw materials of knowledge and mental readiness to use it a similar intricate process of selection and organization intervenes. Education can do nothing but prepare the way for this process. The student himself must carry it on. Like pure religion and undefiled, knowledge is ever a function of the consciousness of the believer. There are no educational sacraments which impart a saving grace. Mechanical education is easy, but it accomplishes only that which should not be accomplished. Real education is hard, for it is a spiritual ministration. The temptation to substitute mere physical manipulation for living interest, spiritual insight, and comprehension ripening into action is the sin which besets us.

Education a life work. According to this view, education is a life process. The individual begins to organize his experience at birth and continues to organize it until he dies. At first the solicitous care of parents attends him; after that comes a long period of watchful direction on the part of teachers. The purpose of this entire ministration is to fit him progressively to undertake this responsibility for himself. The question is sometimes asked, How are the several stages of his education related ? As he passes from the elementary school to the secondary school, and from that to the higher school, and thence into life, how shall we image the journey which he is making or conceive the course which he pursues? In this way, I think:

Let the diagram represent the ladder of life from birth to death; since education is a life process itmay also represent the ladder of education. The space below the first rung is one's preschool experience. Above it comes the elementary-school course, then the secondary-school, and above that the training of the university. The teacher-student relation is common to all these, and if we left the diagram as it stands there would be nothing to indicate a progressive growth in fitness to assume the unaided direction of one's own learning. But draw a diagonal from the bottom of the ladder at the left to the point where the teacher-student relation is represented as ceasing:

Let the spaces to the right of the diagonal represent what the teacher must do and the spaces on the left what the student must do. The student's responsibility grows, and the teacher's directive control gradually disappears. The teacher makeshimself progressively unnecessary. The student little by little learns the process of learning and is at length able to apply it for himself. He has not mastered the *omne scibile* of his day and generation. " All that is knowable " he will never master. That is like the gold at the foot of the rainbow, a pleasing fancy of youth. No one ever searches for it. But"7 to learn to order one's own experiences is a vital J necessity and the workable purpose of education.J

2

SECTION 2

CHAPTER II
WHAT IS KNOWLEDGE?

Mind is " a survival agency" We bring a mind with us when we come here at birth. By it we become aware of our own states and of the world of men and things about us. It seems to exist in order to guide us on our course through life, to be a sort of pilot to help us to make a safe journey. Consequently our awareness has been called " a survival agency." In perfect health one is not reminded that he has internal organs, and in perfect adjustment one is but slightly conscious of an external world. When difficulties arise and this vegetable-like calm is broken, a condition of relatively keen awareness sets, which lasts in some form until the difficulty is disposed of and peace is restored again. This awareness seems to exist to enable the organism to locate its difficulties and to put an end to them I to be valuable in its struggle for life by enabling it to lay hold of or apprehend its world of objects.

We seem also to be born into a world of ready- made things I the earth, the sky, the stars, time and space, the soil, rocks, trees, plants and animals, and,most wonderful of all, our fellow men. All these we find here when we come. To live we must learn to avoid such of them as are harmful, and to lay fast hold upon those which are helpful.

Knowledge, then, is necessary because some things in the universe menace death and others promise life.

Is knowledge contributed by things ? But what sort of a thing is knowledge? And how do we come to have it? The easiest and at the same time the most dangerous answer is that knowledge is due to things making pictures of themselves upon our minds; that perfect knowledge or truth exists when this picturing is complete I when there is perfect agreement between the idea and the object or thing. According to this theory mind is only a rather intricate picture-making device I a kind of sensitive plate. It gets the images of things because they stamp their images upon it. All knowledge is due to the impressions of things. Mind is a *tabula rasa,* upon which the senses write the images of the outer world. To be sure, it is different from a camera with which we take photographs, in that it remembers its past photographs of things and is constantly combining them in strange new ways, so that it is sometimes difficult to tell just which of its pictures are due to the impressions of outer things and which are due to the liberties it has taken in combining them. There are, however,two kinds of true pictures: the direct and the indirectl those which I take myself through the impressions which things make upon my own senses and those which others take and tell me about in some way or other, so that I am able in some measure to copy their copy of the original and make for myself some sort of a picture of it. To be sure, the first-hand knowledge of the world of things is best; but since it is impossible for each one of us to get as much of it as life requires us to have, we must be content to take a large part of it at second hand. This we do by means of books, papers, pictures, maps, music, conversation, instruction, lectures, sermons, etc.

The essence of this theory is that knowledge is given to us by things. They are out there; mind is shut up in here. The senses are the apertures through which they communicate their images. Mind must be passive to get the clearest and truest pictures from outer things. It must present itself clean to the truth which comes to it from outside, or it will mix this truth up and blur it with its own past pictures. Strangely enough, both of the traditional schools of philosophylrealism and absolute idealism I define reality as eternally made existence, and for both of them knowledge-getting can be nothing more than the copying of the object by the idea. Truth is something whose parts areeternally complete. Knowledge is its phantom, its shadow in our minds.

If we have copies only, how can we tell when they are true? Knowledge-getting is thus for these philosophies not a making but a receiving. Truth is an outer something which must come to us. The learner must simply hold the mirror up to the objective world. But if our minds are limited to copies of objects which are outside of them, if all truth is outside and nothing but copies inside the mind, how can it ever find out whether its copies agree with their originals or not ? How can we possibly tell when the picture corresponds with the reality which it professes to picture? On this theory we are forever limited to the picture only; the original is at all times beyond our reach. To tell whether our copy, or picture, is adequate or inadequate, true or false, we must compare it with the thing which it professes to picture, but when we try to do that we get only another copy of the object, not the thing itself. To compare reality with its appearance, we should somehow have to know reality apart from every appearance; and this we cannot do. A true mental picture, or idea, claims to correspond with its object. But so also does a false one. How shall we tell which is which ? If knowledge is merely the copying of the object to be known by the idea which knows it, we never can tell.

What do we know of objects outside of experience ? This theory of what knowledge is will not work, and we must backtrack a bit to find the right path. What right have we to talk about things and truths which are outside of awareness ? Can we say anything or think anything about the things that no one in any way knows | the things that are altogether outside of experience ? If I say the air is peopled with myriads of spirits, you immediately reply: "Not so, for no one has seen them or heard them or in any way communicated with them. Since they have not made themselves known, they are not." But perhaps if you are not a dogmatist you will add the proviso that if they do make themselves known we shall then have to revise this judgment. At any rate, they are not until they are known. It is exactly the same with everything. When my friend tells me that the Washington Elm is no longer standing, I reply, " I saw it but a moment ago as I passed the spot, and I am confident that it is still there and that you are mistaken." If a shipmaster comes into port and announces that an immense island has arisen in a certain quarter of the sea, and other shipmasters who were in the same latitude and longitude at the same time report that they saw no island, we shall have to believe that the first shipmaster is deceiving us and perhaps himself, for the weightof experience would seem to prove that there is no island. When Bishop Berkeley startled mankind by announcing that objects exist only in so far as they are known, it is said that Dr. Johnson vigorously denounced the doctrine; and while arraigning it with his/usual vehemence in the presence of a group of friends one day, he strode majestically up to a stone wall and kicked it, saying as he did so, " This is the way I refute the Bishop's error." But did he refute it ? Did he not instead completely prove the Bishop's contention ? It is only a stone wall that one can kick and feel the kick back from that can really be said to exist. If a man opens his purse to show me that he has a hundred dollars in it and discloses nothing there, I become convinced that his hundred dollars were imaginary. The real hundred dollars must be distinguished from the imaginary hundred dollars, said Immanuel Kant, by the fact that they can be touched and seen, or that we can pass them at the bread shop or the clothing store. Thus experience is the measure of all things, of those that are that they are and of those that are not that they are not, and it is impossible in any way to get outside of experience to find out whether its reports agree with objects, or things-in-themselves, or not. The only world which is or can be is the world within experience.1 No onecan get outside the world of experience to find out whether his ideas accord with things-as-they-are-in- themselves or not. The harder one tries to believe in things-in-themselves, the more certain he becomes that Betsey Prig disposed of them when she uttered " those memorable and tremendous words " to Mrs. Gamp concerning the existence of Mrs. Harris: " I don't believe there 's no sich a person." *The objects we are concerned with are objects as they are experienced.* The object of knowledge is not " absolute truth." Our ideas cannot possibly get into correspondence with things-in-themselves. We are experience-bound and can know things only as they are for mind. Everything that is must enter the subject-object relation. " We can think of matter only in terms of mind," says Herbert Spencer, and Huxley likewise maintained that " all the phenomena of nature are known to us only as facts of consciousness." But this is no doctrine of despair. Just as the dollars that we can heft and see and count and trade for bread and coats are the only real dollars, and the dollars that we cannot pass either upon ourselves or other folks are the imaginary ones, so is it with all the facts and existences of the world. I say there is a study table in my room because I find it there and work upon it. Just at the moment that I do not find it there I shall be compelled to say that it is there no longer.

1" What all *think* we say *is,*" Aristotle, Ethics, Bk. X, Sect. II (Chase's translation).

What is truth ? Truth is a relation which exists between the parts of experience, between idea and idea, and not between idea and thing. It is an ex- perienceable and not an inexperienceable relation. And yet not all experiences are true, and only a small part of those which may assume the truth relation furnish or can furnish knowledge. I repeat the letters of the alphabet, or I pull a rose to pieces. Is either experience true or not true ? You hear me sound the letters and you say, " You have not named them in their order." " But," I reply, " their order was indifferent to me. I am not trying to name them in order." As soon as I try to name them in their order and succeed or fail, the quality of truth or falsity attaches to my act. The clock ticks, the table supports my paper, the ink flows, the temperature of the room remains equable, the rain beats against the windows, a thousand things are going on about me, and yet they are neither true nor false. They are just happenings. They simply are. How shall I name them ? There is one word by which they are commonly designated, though this word has other and very confusing uses. It is the *word facts.* Because they are so utterly useless, these mere happenings have a very singular quality | they are eternally the same. That a fly buzzed, or the clock ticked, or the table was hard, or the temperature was 68 degrees justnow, is an eternal fact. But taken without a context it has not the slightest significance and no truth whatever. But let the ticking of the clock stop or the room become cold, and very soon attention fastens upon these parts of experience for consideration. Has the clock stopped ? Is it too cold here? These are experiences which are either true or false. We listen for the familiar tick. We look at the pendulum. Yes, it is true that the clock has stopped. And the thermometer shows that the temperature is now but 61 degrees. Our surmise is verified. Our belief was true.

Facts, truths, and knowledge. Facts are very profitless things until we use them. When we relate them to purposes they take on meaning and become immensely important. But if it is plain that facts as facts are not truths, is it equally clear that truths as truths are not knowledge? It was true that the clock had stopped and that the room was too cold. Are these truths knowledge ? I have already closed the window and wound the clock. I shall most likely never have occasion to refer to these particular experiences again. Can they then in any legitimate sense be said to furnish knowledge? *Knowledge* is a high and dignified word, with which spells are worked and lives are bought and sold. Would it not be well to attempt to give it a more vital meaning than this ? Let us see.

I have just moved into a new house. There are five thousand books upon the floor and they must all be arranged on the bookshelves in the library. In how many possible ways can we arrange them? We can arrange them according to size, the color of their bindings, the names of their authors, according to subjects or size of type, according to the number of times the word *the* or any other word appears in each, by the number of commas, semicolons, and periods, the number of lines on a page or words in a line, according to weight or the number of times the letter *a* or any other letter is used in each. It seems likely that there are an infinite number of ways in which the books in a library can be arranged. Which of these will be the right or the true way? Is there any one eternally fixed and divinely instituted sole-and-only- correct way of arranging the books in a library? If there is, does any man yet know what it is ? If my books are of various sizes and my shelves of but two or three, I shall have to arrange them according to size. If I bought the books for their bindings, I should undoubtedly arrange them according to a color scheme. But if I use my books by repeatedly consulting them, I must arrange them in such a way that I can find them quickly and easily when I want them. It is certain that I shall not be able to make this arrangement offhand,and very likely, no matter how well I know my books, I shall need to consider the experience that other people who have arranged libraries have put at my disposal in books in which they have recounted it. At any rate, I shall have to arrange and rearrange my books; and it is not likely that I shall ever get them so perfectly classified that the advent of new books and the arising of new needs will not force me to rearrange them. What seems very clear in this undertaking is that the true arrangement is the one which most nearly answers my need | that I find out whether it is true or not only by trying it out, and that in the nature of the case it must constantly undergo revision. It must be noted that our arrangement of the books cannot be a fanciful or purely subjective one. It is in the strictest sense determined by relating the nature of the books to our purpose or need. Now is this true only of books or is it true of all our mentally recorded forms of knowledge? I think it is true of all of them. Take any object | a chair, a table, the sun, a rock, or a man. In how many ways is it possible to view it or take it? Here again the answer is that its abstractly possible relations are infinite in number. Is it one or is it many ? That altogether depends upon your point of view. For the physicist each of these objects is a mass of whirling atoms and each of itsconstituent atoms again is infinitely divisible. " If, as we shall see," says Professor John Cox in his little book " Beyond the Atom," " the mass of an electron is wholly electrical its diameter can be shown to be of the order io'3cm.; that of an atom is io8cm. The electron is thus one hundred thousand times smaller than the atom and the spaces between electrons perhaps one hundred million times the diameter of an electron. This suggests inevitably an arrangement like a planetary system." " Let us consider a ball lying on the ground. In what sense is that ball individuated ? Our main reason for calling it so is its capacity for satisfying our athletic propensities; but whatever else may pertain to matter-in-itself it is clear enough that this quality is not relevant. The ball, however, can be easily lifted from the earth, whereas the molehill near it, resembling it in appearance, would require a spade, if separation is to be effected. This is merely a question of degree of cohesive force. To the Lilliputian the ball would be as completely a part of the earth as the molehill. Imagine also a giant whose body stretched from the Solar System to Sirius and who regarded our whole solar system as a single body; if he were possessed of sufficient analytic power and provided with sufficiently delicate analytical instruments, he might then distinguish sun, earth, and other planets as constituentfactors of that single body. If his sensational apparatus were proportionately coarser than ours from the point of view of their perceptive powers, he would not even appreciate the solar heat as such." 1 Why then do we call things one when they are many? Physical individuation is due to purpose. Whether a thing is one or many depends upon our intention. The word *one* is in our name for the whole I the universe. The lowest term to which we at present reduce it, the electron, is also one, and everything that comes between is either one or many to suit our purpose. Nor is this all. Every one of these ones of our making has some sort of relation to everything else in existence. It is larger or smaller, heavier or lighter, brighter or darker, more active or passive, eastward or westward, similar or dissimilar to everything else there is. The possible relations which any one thing can bear to the rest of existence are infinite in number. If we are for a moment tempted to define knowledge as the comprehension of that which is, we are at once appalled by the absurd presumption of such a notion. The field of possible knowledge lies infinitely extended before the mind, but we are under no temptation to apply the word to any and every relation which consciousness may note in existence. Even the most enthusiastic devotee of originalresearch is not likely to set about examining, describing, and comparing the sands of the seashore for the same reason that he is not likely to set about arranging his books according to the number of times the word *the* is used in each volume. The notion that just any kind of description or classification is science does not work. The realm of knowledge is much smaller than the realm of fact. Take for example this table; from how many different points of view may I look at it ? No one can count them ; but if they could be compassed, the table could conceivably be drawn from every one of them, and every single picture of the table, if it checked up with subsequent pictures of it from the same point of view, would be a true picture of it. Now which one of this infinite number of appearances or aspects of the table is the real table? Is there any one and only true way to draw a table ? May not one sketch it from above or below, from north, northeast, or south, southwest, and still make a true picture of it ? Abstractly one aspect of the table is just as true as another, but not so concretely. Concretely a table is for use, and that aspect of it which presents its use relations the crystallized experience of the race has voted to regard as the preferred aspect, the real table. If you are buying one, you must be careful to get one which fits your intention; if you are drawing one,you must be careful to draw one which fits your intention also. I am not saying that you can draw it as you please any more than you can arrange your books in any way you may fancy. To be sure you can do both these things, only neither the drawing nor the arrangement will be true. When you come to check them up, you will find that future need will not be realized in them; that is, they will not work out the test of truth.

1 Arnold, Scientific Fact and Metaphysical Reality, p. 71. London, 1904.

Is there any object in existence which has always the same color no matter what light may play upon it, always the same shape no matter from what angle or at what distance we may behold it, always the same smoothness no matter how many times we may magnify its surface, always the same resistance no matter what the force that opposes it, which has the same weight at the center of the earth, at its surface, and on a mountain top ? Is there, in short, anything whose qualities do not change with our changing relation to it? If there is anywhere such unchanging thing, to know it will be to think of it in but one way; but in the case of the things that change with our relation to them we must take our choice of the many possible ways of thinking of them, and in that choice we shall be constrained by our need to single out that aspect of them which will give us the largest measure of control over them.

What is it that we name ? A noun, according to the grammar definition, is the name of a particular thing, but this definition is incorrect I there are no words in language which are the names of particular things.   All words, whether verbs, adjectives, adverbs, prepositions, or conjunctions, are nouns in the sense of being names, but no one of them is the name of a percept or a present particular experience. They are all names of *kinds* of things, of classes or concepts. We might have one name for John when he is young and another when he is old; one when he is angry and another for him when he is happy; one name for him when he is asleep and another for him when he is awake; one for him when he is in health and another when he is sick. He is a different person to my different perceptions of him. But for him in all his different moods and conditions I have just one name. Why is this? Would it not be better to give him one name when he is angry and another when he is not angry? He is so very different in the two conditions that I am sometimes led to say that he is two different persons. If language existed for the sake merely of describing happenings, I should have at least two names for him. If knowledge about him consisted merely in the notation of facts, I should have to give a separate name to each different and eternally trueparticular fact about him. Is it, then, for mere economy of utterance that I do not do this, but instead give him one name ? Naming is not for purposes of fact-designating. In a sense it is for purposes of fact-obscuring. We give him one name, which he carries with him through life, which enables us to forget that he is young or old, rich or poor, sick or well, stooped or straight, angry or not angry, honest or dishonest, honorable or dishonorable. Would it not be better if we named noble men by noble names and ignoble ones by ignoble names, so that the whole world would at once know how to take them ? Not so. That one aspect which the whole world must note in dealing with them is just that they are human beings, and as such they must be taken, so we give them proper names, the names proper to human beings, which of themselves indicate nothing as to the facts of their past lives, nothing as to what we must expect of them except the greatest fact of all I that they are just human beings, the particulars of whose action we can anticipate best, not by being at once made aware of what they have done or what so-called traits of character they possess, but just by approaching them with the uncertainty and expectancy which belongs only to undiscovered but generally known objects. When conditions arise under which all the members of a human group must be treated alike,as in a prison or for certain purposes in the army, their proper names are for these purposes overlooked, and they are all reduced to the level of numbers. It is conceivable that we shall grow in grace to the extent of disregarding nationality and ancestral religious differences in our naming of human beings, and that difference of sex may in time not be regarded as so fundamental a human consideration as to require a separate form of proper name for its indication. At any rate, real sex equality can hardly exist until human equality registers itself as the more fundamental fact in our scheme of formulating our anticipations.

Have proper names always belonged to human animals? The first act or work that Adam is represented as performing was the naming of the animals. " And out of the ground the Lord God formed every beast of the field, and every fowl of the air; and brought them unto Adam to see what he would call them: and whatsoever Adam called every living creature, that was the name thereof." Yet it is certain that these Adamic names did not stick, and that the first and the continuing social work which every child of Adam has ever since had to perform is to rename the animals and all the objects in his world of experience. What kinds of names did Adam give them ? Proper names or common names ? . It is certain that for perhapsthousands of years only the men of power and their associates had particular, or proper, names; the insignificant ones had none. In historic and even in very recent days slaves had no proper names. In exceptional cases, that is, when in some way or other expectation singled them out for peculiar attention, they earned names. To the oft-repeated query " What's in a name ? " we must reply, therefore, "A whole philosophy and much of the history of the race." An object is named not because it is an object or a fact, but because of our expectation as to its future I because of our anticipation of further experience of it. The name we give it is only our designation of our intention with regard to it, our indication of our plan to use it or act toward it in the way the name indicates. Relatively few of the animals attain proper names, and inanimate objects seldom are honored with them. But sometimes they secure such a hold upon our attention that we can no longer treat them adequately if we refer to them merely as instances of their kind. They must be promoted to something like an equality of consideration with ourselves. Thus, by a strange inversion, human beings are under certain conditions deprived of proper names, and animals and even inanimate objects are given them; but it is our desire to accord special treatment to both of them, not only now but during the prospectiveperiod of our contact with them that causes us to give or take away their individual names. Like the king or the college, we confer a title not merely to register the fact that we conceive that the recipient has deserved it, but at the same time we call upon all mankind, and most especially pledge ourselves, to accord to them all the privileges, rights, immunities, honors, to which they are *entitled.* Thus names are primarily scaffoldings from which we would build our future acts.

Why do we name kinds of things rather than things taken individually ? Most animals and inanimate objects we do not find ourselves constrained to honor with particular names. We act and react to them best, both mentally and muscularly, by naming them by their *kinds.* This dog, this gun, this bird, this circle, this wagon, as an existence, to be sure, is different from every other existence of its kind; but every dog is an object to beware of or pet and make friends with, and every gun is an object to shoot with and to handle carefully; hence one name will do for them all. Sensory experience is wide and full of variety, but motor reactions are narrow in range, and repetition is their characteristic. We name these things whose particularity is nothing to us, not for what they are but for what we do or can do with them. " It is evident," says Professor Baldwin, " that the ' general' or ' abstract'is not a content at all. It is an attitude, an expectation, a motor tendency. It is the possibility of a reaction which will answer equally for a great many particular experiences." " All general ideas," says Professor Royce, " are the mental aspects of habits of response in presence of those general characters of things to which the ideas in question relate. Without motor habits, no ideas." The sensory system is like the mouth of the funnel; the motor system is its narrow neck. Hence the value of reducing things to kinds. It is what we do with the object that we name. Knowledge comes through conceptualizing, through locating meanings, but to get it we must disregard all particularity of facts about the object and cleave fast to its significance. Again, it is our purpose which determines which of its many possible meanings we shall choose. Whenever our purpose involves more than casual dealings with dogs, guns, or automobiles, we must handle them under subclasses. The breeder's knowledge of dogs must be different from the veterinarian's; the maker's knowledge of the automobile must be different from the user's.

Does knowing anything mean the ability to use it in all possible ways? It has various meanings; we must choose those that minister to our needs. Here is an object which I picked up from the ground near the Pyramid of the Sun in Mexico.As nearly as I can tell, no one knows what it is, though such objects are common in that country. It is made of burnt clay, is round and of about two inches in diameter, is ornamented, and has a small hole in the center. It has a certain weight, which I can determine. I can also learn many other things *about* it. But still I say I do not know what it is. If I knew the name of the ancient Indian who made it or the process by which he made it, I should still be dissatisfied with my knowledge about it. What is it I want to know before I can say that I know it ? Simply its use. Professor James divided knowledge into two kinds|knowledge *about* things and knowledge *of* things. The knowledge of things is knowledge of use. Without it the rest is mere description. It alone enables me in imagination to sit down in the seat of the ancient Indian and take this object in my hand, and in thought to refer it to its place in a possible scheme of things. It alone has the forward look | the relation to purpose that all real knowledge must have to distinguish it from merely mental lumber out of which homes could be built if we only had plans with which to shape them. Use alone furnishes the organizing principle which g1ves the related facts significance and welds them into a system.

Wttat ts the cause of anything? We sometimes say that to know things is to know their *causes,*but the causes of things are numerous. " The whole state of the universe is ultimately responsible for any given result." The real cause of anything is the sum total of existence, and Tennyson was speaking literally as well as poetically when he declared to the flower in the crannied wall that to know it is to know what God and man is. Yet we shall save our souls from scholasticism on the one hand and from whatever bargains we may make with the devil on the other by learning at last, as Faust did, that life and mind find the satisfaction of reality only in helping the peasants to save their fields.

What we denominate the cause of anything is inextricably mixed up with our own purposes and suffused with our own energies. It is that phase of the sum total of the conditions of its existence which we select because of its future reference, not to the reenactment of the thing, but as affording us the peculiar form of control over the thing that we are for the time being seeking. Causes, like every other form of knowledge, are therefore full of relativity. Here is a case of typhoid fever. What caused it? The whole state and condition of the patient, together with his past acts and a chain of ancestral conditions stretching out to infinity, have conspired together to bring this particular person just at this particular moment to his sick bed.Why do we dismiss all the rest and say that the typhoid fever is undoubtedly due to his drinking polluted water or milk? Other members of his family have partaken of the same water or the same milk; yet they are not sick. It must be, therefore, that his sickness is due to the fact that he was in a depressed condition of being, that his bodily resistance was low and theirs perhaps was not. His organism was hospitable to the bacteria that are ever seeking guest privileges from us, and theirs were not. Why do we not say, then, that typhoid fever is caused by a poor condition of resistance on the part of the human organism and not by polluted water or milk ? The answer would seem to be that bodily resistance is by no means so controllable a factor or so removable a condition as the purification of the water or the milk. We name *them* the cause rather than z'/, for the reason that we can take hold by that particular handle and lift the burden more easily than we can by any other of its innumerable handles. Right here we have an excellent illustration of the fact that what we call the cause of a happening is a function of our activity and not of the thing in itself | that causes are unitable with experience and not preexistent and forever fixed, and that our obligation to them is to find them in terms of control and not in terms of their absolute being. It is this: Inoculationis now employed as a preventive of typhoid fever. Suppose that of a group of say six soldiers or six travelers, five have taken the precaution to be inoculated before setting out on the campaign or on the journey. They drink of the same water and the same milk, and the sixth one contracts typhoid fever. The others do not. What shall we say *caused* his typhoid fever? The polluted water or milk? or a low general state of resistance? or the fact that he had not taken the precaution which the others took? Undoubtedly the last; and if, in the development of medical experience of this disease, it shall be found that this precaution works, then failure to employ it, and not the taking of polluted water or milk, or a low general state of bodily resistance, will be singled out as *the cause* of the disease. This same human partiality as determined by purpose operates in the singling out of causes in every other field of experience. A stone falls and hits the earth. Why did it fall ? The force of gravitation caused it to. But no; the force of gravitation has been acting upon it for centuries, and it fell but now. Someone must have thrown it. That may be, but there is no one whom I can find near. Then its fall must have been caused by the fact that it was insecurely propped up above the earth's surface. And under like conditions it will fall again. Thus we work through all the range of experienceablepossibility until we come upon the reenactable factor which would produce the result we seek, and, having found it, we say it is *the cause*. As a matter of fact, *it* is not *the* cause. The causes are so many that, if we attempt to describe them, we shall be utterly lost in bewilderment and confusion. But it is *the* cause that we are seeking, for our *seeking* is a singling and orders the confusion.

Plato's doctrine that knowledge is not description but the pursuit of that which makes men better. It is the definiteness of purpose which the seeker brings that results in knowledge. And this is a very old, though a commonly disregarded, doctrine. Do you remember how, in the tenth book of Plato's " Republic," having worked out the principles of comprehension, he returns to a consideration of the poets and his reasons for denying that they should be the educators of mankind ? They hold the mirror up to nature, and that is an easy way to get the seeming images of things, but they are satisfied with appearances only. " Hence we must inquire whether the poets are mere imitators, who have so far imposed upon the spectators that when they behold their performances, they fail to perceive that these productions are twice removed from reality, and easily worked out by a person unacquainted with the truth because they are phantoms, and not realities." " Concerning those grandest and mostbeautiful subjects which Homer undertakes to treat, such as war, and the conduct of campaigns, and the administration of cities, and the education of man, it is surely just to institute an inquiry, and ask the question, thus: ' My dear Homer, if you are really only once removed from the truth, instead of being twice removed and the manufacturer of a phantom, according to our definition of an imitator; and if you used to be able to distinguish between the pursuits which make men better or worse, in private and public; tell us what city owes a better constitution to you, as Sparta owes hers to Lycurgus, and as many cities, great and small, owe theirs to other legislators ? What state attributes to you the benefits derived from a good code of laws ?' . . . Does the story go that any war in Homer's time was brought to a happy termination under his command, or by his advice ? Is he reputed to have been . . . the author of a number of ingenious inventions bearing upon the useful arts or other practical matters, which would show that he was a man of wisdom in the affairs of life ? . . . Or did he personally conduct the education of disciples who benefited society and teach mankind a way of life ?" ". . . Does the painter understand how the bit and bridle ought to be shaped ? Is it not the case that even the makers, the smith and the saddler, are ignorant on this subject, and only therider who knows how to use the things in question knows and understands it ? ... The imitative person knows nothing of importance about the things which he imitates, and therefore imitation is an amusement and not a serious business." Knowing, then, for Plato arises from use and is for use.

But the heart of Plato's pragmatism is found in a passage in the Euthydemus: "'And what knowledge ought we to acquire ?' May we not answer with absolute truth |' A knowledge which will do us good' ? ' Certainly,' he said.

" And should we be any the better if we went about having a knowledge of the places where most gold was hidden in the earth ? ' Perhaps we should,' he said.

"' But have we not already proved,' I said,' that we should be none the better off, even if without trouble and digging all the gold which there is in the earth were ours ? And if we knew how to convert stones into gold the knowledge would be of no value to us, unless we knew how to use the gold ? Do you not remember ?' I said,' I quite remember,' he said.

"' Nor would any other knowledge, whether of money-making, or of medicine, or of any other art which knows only how to make a thing, and not to use it when made, be of any good to us. Am I not right ?' He agreed.

" ' And if there were a knowledge which was able to make men immortal, without giving them the knowledge of the way to use the immortality, neither would there be any use in that, if we may argue from the analogy of the previous instances ?' To all this he agreed.

"' Then, my dear boy,' I said, ' the knowledge which we want is one that uses as well as makes.'"l

1 Plato, Euthydemus (Jowett's translation), 288, 289.

3

SECTION 3

CHAPTER III
  THE DOCTRINE OF GENERAL DISCIPLINE1
  What this doctrine has cost and why it sticks. If knowledge-getting is the wise and purposeful selection from the infinity of facts and relations which exist of those which make a serious difference to life, it would seem that education owes its greatest duty to that process. But no, says one army of educators; education's first duty is to form and not to inform the mind. This is the centuries-old doctrine of formal discipline. Of it we are indeed justified in complaining, as did John of Salisbury of the Nominalist-Realist controversy which absorbed the scholars of his day, that " more time has been consumed [by it] than the Ceesars gave to the conquest and dominion of the globe, more money wasted than Croesus counted in all his wealth."

We are told in the Scriptures that we should not put new wine into old wine skins, lest the wine skins burst and the wine be spilled, but there is another and even a better reason I the old wineskins are not sanitary. They contain the elements of decay. The new wine that goes into them will be poisoned, and we who drink of it will die. Nevertheless, this pouring of new wine into old bottles is one of the chief activities of education. This is due, it would seem, to the fact that those who so zealously pour their life work in the service of education into the old and time-infected wine skins of formal discipline have no other bottles into which to pour it. Strangely enough, even that hardy company of critics who a few years ago set about liberating the spirit of youth from the contamination of this process did its work so imperfectly that the more unthinking lovers of the old bottles still conceive themselves to be justified in using them. Indeed, they are reassured by a belief that " recent careful investigations have shown that there is much in the doctrine of formal discipline." Nothing could be farther from the truth. But the critics of the doctrine, rather than its friends, are to blame for this, for they have stated their findings in such a way as to invite just this misuse of them. When Herbart undertook to reform psychology by casting out the hypostatized entities called faculties of the mind, which scholastic ignorance, traditionalized by centuries, had erected to explain mental life, he made the mistake of continuing to use the old terminology of faculties to designate the new-foundactivities which came to light when he tore away the scholastic rubbish. The result of his thus putting his new wine into old words was that it took the learned world half a century to discover that the wine was new, it tasted so like the old; and though nearly a century has now elapsed, the bulk of mankind has not yet discovered that it tastes and is different. Old words and phrases do not work well as provokers of new ideas. We shall not learn to think clearly about the behavior of mind until we cease to use such phrases as *the intellect, the will, the emotions, the observation, the imagination, the memory, the reason,* etc. in our discussions, and begin with one accord to talk about knowing, willing, feeling, imagining, remembering, reasoning, instead. The acts we know and can recognize, but that there are mental organs set apart for the performance of each one of them, as the eyes are for seeing, the ears for hearing, and the teeth for chewing, though it is an old doctrine, is not a true one. And now nearly a hundred years after it was found out to be untrue by the psychologists, this phrenology of mind is still a ruling superstition of education, and the implicit basis of a very large and important part of current educational theory and practice. We shall not learn to think clearly about education until we cease to becloud ourselves by using the word *discipline,*

1 For an extended discussion of this subject, see Thorndike, Educational Psychology, Vol. II (Teachers College, New York), and Heck, Mental Discipline (John Lane Company, New York).

What is tlie doctrine of formal discipline? It seems to be an exceedingly elusive and slippery affirmation I a series of running changes to escape its critics, and of shifting meanings assumed one after the other to withstand the attacks which have been made upon it. There is no way to corner it and make it tell what it means and what it does not mean save by quoting the documents which discuss it. Writing in 1867, Professor Youmans has this to say about it: " The friends of educational improvement maintain that the system of culture which prevails in our higher institutions of learning, and which is limited chiefly to the acquisition of the mathematics, and of the ancient languages and literature, was shaped years ago in a state of things so widely different from the present that it has become inadequate to existing requirements. . . . As man is a being of action, it is demanded that his education shall be a preparation for action. As the highest use of knowledge is for guidance, it is insisted that our collegiate establishments shall give a leading place to those subjects of study which will afford a better preparation for the duties and work of the age in which we live. The adherents of the traditional system reply that all this is but the unreasoning clamor of a restless and innovating age, which wholly misconceives the true aim of higher culture and would reduce everything to thestandard of a low and sordid utility. They maintain that knowledge is to be acquired not on account of its capability of useful application, but for its own intrinsic interest; that the purpose of a liberal education is not to prepare for a vocation or profession, but to train the intellectual faculties. They therefore hold that *Mental Discipline* is the true object of a higher culture, and that for its attainment the study of" the ancient classics and mathematics is superior to all other means." 1 " Throughout our discussion thus far," writes Dr. Noah Porter in his " American Colleges and the American Public,"2 " we have assumed that certain studies may be of the greatest value for discipline which possess no other obvious and direct utility." And again: " But even on the theory that many studies are valuable chiefly as a gymnastic l' the *grindstone* theory,' as Mr. Atkinson calls it I it deserves to be considered whether the mathematics are not carried too far for their highest efficiency in a general course; whether excessive tediousness and painful drudgery are not sometimes the effect of driving a class into too minute calculations or vexing them with manifold problems." But Dr. Porter's enthusiasm for " the grindstone theory" as applied to the classics shows no such abatement. " Unless it can bedecisively proved that the so-called useful studies are as efficient in their disciplinary capacity and effect, it forms no objection to a study that its acquisitions cannot be used." There is competent testimony as to its presence in Germany also, for the present emperor in speaking of the defenders of the existing program in the classical gymnasia in 1892 said, " If anyone enters into a discussion with these gentlemen on this point and attempts to show him that a young man ought to be prepared, to some extent at least, for life and its manifest problems, they will tell him that such is not the function of the school, its principal aim being the discipline, or gymnastic, of the mind, and that if this gymnastic were properly conducted, the young man would be capable of doing all that is necessary in life." 1, That this particular claim for certain studies has not been abandoned by our present-day molders of educational opinion is made plain by Professor Shorey in the volume entitled " Latin and Greek in American Education "2: " Throughout this discussion I have taken for granted the general belief of educators, statesmen, and the man in the street, from Plato and Aristotle to John Stuart Mill, Faraday, Lincoln, President Taft, and Anatole France, that there is such a thing as intellectual discipline, and somestudies are a better mental gymnastic than others. This, like other notions of ' common sense' is subject to all due qualifications and limitations. But it is now denied altogether, and the authority of Plato, Mill, Faraday, or Lincoln is met by the names of O'Shea, Bagley, Home, Thorndike, Bolton, and De Garmo. Tastes in authorities differ." This is a singular, and by no means an edifying, method of arriving at a proper understanding of the point at issue. Would that Professor Shorey had confined himself to a discussion of " the due qualifications and limitations" to which this common-sense notion must be subjected.

1 Youmans, The Culture demanded by Modern Life, p. 2. New York, 1867.

2 New Haven, 1870.

1 Henderson, Principles of Education, p. 289. New York, 1910. 3 The Macmillan Company. New York, 1911.

The harm that the doctrine works. The tragic aspect of the doctrine of formal discipline is that it is handed down by the colleges to the lower schools, and infects pretty completely all forms of education. Little children in the elementary grades are required to study much arithmetic that is archaic, much grammar that is useless, much history that they do not understand, and much spelling that they will never again have occasion for, for the reason that these things forsooth develop and discipline the mind. One by one in high schools and colleges this doctrine takes the new studies into its net, and little by little transforms them into apathy- breeding, mind-destroying treadmills. It is not an adjective that belongs to studies; it is a false use

to which studies are put. Any body of knowledge may be taught from the standpoint of formal discipline. Its real human worth may be largely neglected, and a use which quite obscures its value may be sought in it. Some of the earlier champions of science as a school study made the mistake of commending it on the ground that it disciplines the mind as genuinely as the classics or mathematics do, and as a result science is very generally taught as formal discipline. So is manual training, so is literature, and so may history, commercial branches, domestic science, and even shop work be taught, unless we guard against this debasing of them. The statement is frequently made that it makes no difference what you study so long as you study it well. If the content is of no significance whatever, as this statement implies, it must be the mental discipline and nothing else which gives the study value. Is it, then, any wonder that Mr. Dooley was constrained to reword this position to the effect that " it makes no difference what you study so long as you hate it"?

The history of this doctrine. Let us glance at the history of this doctrine. As nearly as I can discover, it was Plato who first began to talk of principles in the soul, and in one place in the " Republic " he defines faculties as " powers in us, and in all other things, by which we do as we do. Sight and hearingI should call faculties. ... In speaking of a faculty I think only of its sphere and its result." 1 Plato throughout his writings is struggling with the impossibility of making an old language lend itself to the needs of radically new ways of thinking, and must by no means be held to that literal definite- ness of imagery and meaning which subsequent thinkers have put into his conceptions. There is nothing, however, that I can find in his writings that leads to the belief that the book which Rousseau called " the finest treatise on education ever written " in any sentence propounds the doctrine of formal discipline. On the contrary, Plato's whole energy is devoted to emphasizing the overwhelming importance of the content of instruction. It is for that reason and for none other that he calls for the reediting of the poets. It is for that reason that he describes the perfect literary education after this fashion: " Even so, as I maintain, neither we nor our guardians whom we have to educate, can ever become musical until we and they know the essential forms of temperance, courage, liberality, magnificence, and their kindred, as well as the contrary forms in all their combinations, and can recognize them and their images wherever they are found, not slighting them either in small things or in great, but believing them all to be within the sphere ofone art and study. " 1 By *essential forms*2 Plato means the " ideas." The Platonic ideas are the clear concepts or definitions which Plato's master, Socrates, had spent his life in searching for. Here, at any rate, they are concepts or ideas of the mind. In this and the other dialogues he defines them from the standpoint of mental content, as, for example : Courage is the preserving " under all circumstances that opinion about the nature of things to be feared and not to be feared in which our legislator educated them." 3 " Temperance ... is the ordering or controlling of certain pleasures and desires."4 "It would seem, Adeimantus, that the direction in which education starts a man, will determine his future life." 5 " To the rulers, then, it is the first and greatest commandment of God, that there shall be nothing of which they shall be such good guardians and which they shall watch so intensely as the children, for what they find to be mingled in their souls."6 " Then you are to conceive that we, too, were doing something like this, so far as we were able, when we were selecting oursoldiers and training them in music and gymnastic; you must suppose that we were devising nothing else than how with full conviction our men might best take the color of the laws, like a dye, in order that their opinion both about terrors and about all else, might turn out indelible, because their quality and their nurture had been appropriate; and that the detergents of the soul, however fatal in their operation, might never wash away their dye, whether pleasure, more tremendous in its efficiency than any niter or alkali, or pain and fear and desire, stronger than all other detergents. It is this faculty, a safekeeping through everything of the right and lawful opinion with regard to what is terrible and what is not, which I name and set down as courage, unless you say something against it." l

1 Republic (Jowett's translation), 477.

1 Republic (Jowett's translation), 402.

a What Plato means by this alphabet of life which he declares we must know as thoroughly as our A B C's, is I think made clear by answering the question, What are the essential forms of geometry?

8 Republic (Jowett's translation), 429.

4 Ibid. 430.

6 Ibid. 425.

' Republic (Bosanquet's translation), 415.

Plato's theory of crime is " that the most gifted minds, when they are ill educated, become preeminently bad. Do not great crimes and the spirit of pure evil spring out of a fullness of nature ruined by education rather than from any inferiority, whereas weak natures are scarcely capable of any very great good or very great evil ? " 2 Education has no need to strengthen or develop or form such minds; they are strong by nature; but the " classical education which the Greeks got by the study of Homer andHesiod " is not sufficient to put their feet in the way of life. The whole burden of Plato's criticism is that the content of the instruction upon which the Greeks relied was unsatisfactory. Even the idea of the good, the loftiest of all the mind's conceptions, is a mental content. " And the soul is like the eye; when resting upon that on which truth and being shine, the soul perceives and understands and is radiant with intelligence."l

1 Republic (Bosanquet's translation), 430.

2 Republic (Jowett's translation), 491.

But, you are perhaps saying, that is all very well; nevertheless, when Plato came to outline his scheme of higher education he chose his subjects of study not for the sake of their content but because of their disciplinary value. It is true that he speaks of education many times as the process of directing the mind to " that upon which truth and being shine," that he would have Homer banished because his ideas are so misinforming, that he would supervise every kind of artist and image maker so that only the breezes of beauty and health should blow over the children; but see if he does not work out another conception of education than that it is the process of bringing the mind into contact with a profitable environment, when he discusses the subjects of the higher course of study. That course begins when the youth is twenty years of age. It lasts for fifteen years, the first ten of which are to be spent upon arithmetic, geometry, astronomy, and music, and the last five in the study of dialectic. Why does Plato want them to study these subjects?

1 Republic (Jowett's translation), 508.

First, there are four degrees of knowledge, and they form a ladder by which the soul may climb to the comprehension of the highest form of being | the comprehension of the *good*. We are invited to take a line and divide it into two unequal parts, thus:

The invisible
world

The visible
world

then to divide each of these parts in the same proportion; and to suppose that these main divisions represent one the world of sense, or the visible world, and the other the world of intelligence, or the invisible world. Then we are asked to compare the subdivisions of each in respect to their clearness or want of clearness. We may know the things of the visible world either directly by seeing and sensing them ourselves, or indirectly by seeing pictures of them, reflections of them in mirrors, or in maps, descriptions, etc. This second kind of knowledge is less clear than the first, so it must be put below it in the first of the subdivisions of our diagram. Let us speak of this lowest kind of knowledge as the perception of shadows or copies. Above it will come the world of visible objects which we know by faith. In the lower form of knowledge of the invisible world we are concerned with things not seen, such as lines, points, circles, numbers, etc. These thoughts are suggested by things, but we get them only by abstracting one aspect from out the mass of qualities which unite to make up any object. These studies teach us to make those abstractions, to think about thoughts, not in general but in connection with a particular subject matter. The peculiarity of this kind of knowledge is that it assumes that there are lines and points and numbers, and proceeds to draw such inferences as it can from the assumption that they exist. The highest kind of knowledge inquires into the nature of these assumptions. It refuses to be hypothetical, but starting from certainty it advances to certainty through certainty. The hypothetical knowledge of geometry and arithmetic and such like studies is the work of understanding. And pure science unaided by hypothesis is the work of reason. Now we may fill the several spaces in our diagram:

The invisible
world

Reason

Understanding
The visible
world

Faith
Perception
Science or knowledge
Hypothetical knowledge
Objects or things
Shadows

The training in music and gymnastic has informed us concerning the knowledge of the visible world. It remains for the higher education to inform us concerning the intelligible world. We begin with arithmetic, which is " a something which all the arts and sciences and intelligences use in common and which everyone first has to learn among the elements of education." 1 It is a study which leads to reflection. " Its true use is simply to draw the soul towards being."2 " We must endeavor to persuade those who are to be the principal men of our state to go and learn arithmetic,not as amateurs, but they must carry on the study until they see the nature of numbers with the mind only."1 Some of the things of sense do not invite us to think, while in the case of other objects the senses give us such untrustworthy reports that further inquiry is imperatively necessary. Sight cannot adequately perceive greatness and smallness, thickness and thinness, hardness and softness. Sense reports the same thing now as hard, now as soft, now as light, now as heavy; the soul must summon intelligence and calculation that she may know whether the several objects announced to her are two or one. When some contradiction is " always present, and one is the reverse of one, and involves the conception of plurality, then thought begins to be aroused within us, and the soul, perplexed and wanting to arrive at a decision, asks ' What is absolute unity ?' This is the way in which the study of the one has a power of drawing and converting the mind to the contemplation of true being."2 Arithmetic compels the soul to reason about abstract numbers. For that reason it has a great and elevating effect. The mental operations which it invites us to perform are valuable forms of learning, but they must be supplemented by practice in learning the specificoperations of geometry, which are different, as well as those of astronomy and of music. Plato does not claim for any one of these that they teach us to think, but only that they teach us to think arithmetically, geometrically, astronomically, and concerning music. No one of them is enough, and taken all together they are by no means enough. " All this is but the prelude to the actual strain that we have to learn. For you surely would not regard the skilled mathematician as a dialectician ? Assuredly not, he said: I have hardly ever known a mathematician who was capable of reasoning." 1 Dialectic, then, which is the art of asking and answering questions, must be pursued for five years; and even this is not enough, for those who study it must keep on educating themselves as long as they live.

1 Republic (Jowett's translation), 522.

2 Ibid. 523.

1 Republic (Jowett's translation), 525.

2 Ibid. 524 (absolute unity = unity itself).

But if the pursuit of each of these studies contributes only its quotum of specific knowledge, what about such statements as that " even the dull, if they have had an arithmetical training, although they may derive no other advantage from it, always become much quicker than they would otherwise have been,"2 and " as experience proves, anyone who has studied geometry is infinitely quicker of apprehension than one who has not" ?3 Are

1 Republic (Jowett's translation), 531. 3 Ibid. 526. " Ibid. 527.

they quickened because their minds have been sharpened and they have been trained to think? But Plato himself employs the statement, " I have hardly ever known a mathematician who was capable of reasoning." It must therefore be that they have been quickened in some other way. In what other way could they have been quickened ? My little girl does not know how to read, but she studies reading. I notice a great change in her. Before, when I asked her to look at a book she did so indifferently; now she takes it with alacrity. She has learned a new thought of herself; she is one who can find out things from books. Her alacrity is not there because her mind as a mind has been developed and is now a more perfect mind than it was before. It is due to the fact that she has found a specific method of attack, that she has learned how to use her mind and in one way found out that she can accomplish something by using it.1

Plato does not leave us so uncertain as this even as to what he regards as the task of education and what his definition of education is. He is very definite about it. Hear him: " But then, if I am right, certain professors of education must be wrong when they say that they can put a knowledge into the soul which was not there before," as one might speak of inserting sight into eyes which have it not. " Whereas our argument shows that the power and capacity of learning exists in the soul already."1 Shall we consider in what way our guardians are to be produced ? " The process, I said, ... is the turning round of a soul passing from a day which is little better than night to the true day of being." 2 That is, neither knowledge nor powers nor capacities which are not there already can be inserted in the soul from outside. The whole and sole business of education consists in directing the mind or turning it to the consideration of that which is important.

1 That this is Plato's conception is, I think, borne out by the passage in 411 of the " Republic," in which he describes the ill effect of an education in gymnastic alone as follows : " And what happens if he do nothing else, and holds no converse with the Muses, does not even that intelligence which there may be in him, having no taste of any sort of learning or inquiry or thought or culture, grow feeble and dull and blind, his mind never waking up or receiving nourishment and his senses not being purged of their mists?" (Jowett's translation).

Now though Aristotle, the great classifier, crystallized the different kinds of functioning of the soul into a somewhat more hard and fast doctrine of faculties, he did not speak of education as existing to form or develop them. He did say in the " Psychology " that " if imagination means the power whereby what we call a phantasm is awakened in us, and if our use of language is not merely metaphorical, then imagination is one of those faculties or mental forces in us by virtue of which we judge and are capable of truth and error. And those faculties include sensation, opinion, scientific knowledge, and reasoning."1 But when he discusses education, his emphasis is wholly upon the impressions which play upon us in our earliest years. He agrees with his master, Plato, that the selection of the environment is education's main task. " Virtue," for him, " consists in rejoicing and loving and hating aright"2; that is, in knowing what things to love and what things to hate. " The virtues we get by first performing single acts of working, which, again, is the case of other things, as the arts for instance; for what we have to make when we have learned how, these we learn how to make by making. ... In one word, the habits are produced from the acts of working like to them: and so what we have to do is to give a certain character to these particular acts, because the habits formed correspond to the differences of these. So then, whether we are accustomed this way or that straight from childhood, makes not a small but an important difference, or rather I would say it makes all the difference." 3

1 Republic (Jowett's translation), 518.

2 Ibid. 521.

1 Aristotle, Psychology, in Rand's The Classical Psychologists, p. 68.

2 Politics, VIII, 5.

8 Aristotle, Ethics (Chase's translation), Bk. II, Sect. I.

Even the Romans, who did so much to pervert the wisdom of the Greeks, seem to have taken the Greek notion of education as the process of bringing the mind of the learner into contact with the body of usable knowledge and letting him master it for himself as the proper conception of the teacher's function. In one place in the " Institutes of Oratory" Quintilian distinctly refers to the doctrine of formal discipline only to turn his back to it and to find other and better reasons for the practice which he recommends. This is the passage: " As to geometry, people admit that some attention to it is of advantage in tender years; for they allow that the thinking powers are excited, and the intellect sharpened by it and that a quickness of perception is thence produced; but they fancy that it is not like other sciences profitable after it has been acquired, but only whilst it is being studied. Such is the common opinion respecting it. But it is not without reason that the greatest men have bestowed extreme attention on this science; for as geometry is divided between numbers and figures, the knowledge of numbers assuredly is necessary not only to an orator, but to everyone who has been initiated even in the rudiments of learning.. . . The knowledge of linear figures, too, is frequently required in causes; for law-suits occur concerning boundaries and measures. But geometry has a stillgreater connection with the art of oratory Geometry proves what follows from what precedes, what is unknown from what is known; and do we not draw similar conclusions in speaking? ... Of all proofs, the strongest are what are called geometrical demonstrations, and what does oratory make its object more indisputably than proof ?"1

As nearly as I can discover, this view held throughout the Dark Ages and the Middle Ages, and even when scholasticism flourished with all its metaphysical refinements it was usable knowledge, or what passed for usable knowledge, which was the object of all instruction. Such was certainly the case in the Renaissance and in its Germanized child I the Reformation. The knowledge of the languages was necessary for the sake of purified religion. " They are the scabbard which holds the sword of the spirit."

But when the Renaissance and the Reformation had been accomplished and new conditions brought new needs, the practice of education could not change rapidly enough to meet them. And so bad reasons had to be found for continuing to do that which was nevertheless done from habit and tradition. The schools of the Jesuits may have done something to shape the new justification which was found for continuing the old studies, but Latin was to them the language of a living religion, and they were under no such need to find reasons for their devotion to it as were Protestant schoolmasters. When Luther and his co-reformers sought to give the people of Germany a new religion by breaking away from the Latin Church, why did they not also break away from the Latin language and the traditional education? By doing so they would have made their separation more complete. The answer is found in the words of Melancthon, the organizer of the reformation school system: " Upon the parents, therefore, and upon the community falls the common obligation of the education of the youth of your city. In the first place, they must take care that religion be rightly taught, and this implies as a necessary condition sound instruction in letters." 1

1 Quintilian (Watson's translation), Institutes of Oratory, Bk. I, chap. x.

The Reformation rode in on the great wave of humanism. The reformers were humanists and were bitterly opposed to the medieval education whose chief study was logic. Scholastic Latin, scholastic disputing, and scholastic theology, in short the studies and methods of the scholastics, were all hateful to them. Not the Latin spoken by clerks, which had kept itself alive through the Dark Ages by adapting itself as a living language

1 Melancthon, Inaugural Address at Nuremberg, 1526, in Woodward's Contributions to the History of Education, p. 224. Cambridge, 1906.

to the needs of men, but Latin of classical purity and a learning that enabled the scholar to leap over the ages of confusion back to the pure doctrine contained in the source books of Christianity, became their ideal of education. Indeed, we may say that it was the Reformation which by refusing to have anything to do with the living Latin which had grown up through the ages of the Church made Latin a dead language.

Humanistic Latin it continued to study because of its value to religion, since a large part of the literature of early Christianity had been written in it. But the growth of the native language, the rapid institutionalizing of the new religion, the claims of everyday life, and the increasing pressure of new studies which began to be shaped by vital interests took the heart out of the reformers' reasons for studying the classics. Luther and Melanc- thon had urged these studies upon the people in words which indicate that they aspired to make every man his own reformer of religion. This ambitious use of the classics in time ceased to be the active hope of the schoolmasters, and about the middle of the eighteenth century the German teachers of the old subjects begin to defend their work against the attacks upon it by the exponents of the new realistic studies, by the justification that they train the faculties of the mind.

Thomas Aquinas, Hobbes, and Christian Wolff in their writings made frequent reference to the faculties of the soul. Francis Bacon, in Section 974 of the Natural History, says that " the brains of some creatures, when their heads are roasted, taken in wine, are said to strengthen the memory: as the brains of hares, brains of hens, brains of deers, etc." And speaking of the lack which he found in the exercises used in the universities, he wrote, " It is ever a true rule in exercises that they be framed as near as may be to the life of practice, for otherwise they do pervert the motions and faculties of the mind, and not prepare them." 1

Among the impediments to natural philosophy he notes the promises with which " light and vain men partly from credulity, partly from craft, have loaded the human race, offering promulgation of life, delay of infirmity, relief from pain, supply of natural defects, deceptions of the senses, the binding or inciting of the affections, illuminations of the mental powers, ecstasies, transmuting of substances, etc."2 .

John Locke (1632-1704) is sometimes referred to as the chief exponent of the theory that the true function of education is to develop the powers or faculties of the mind. " The business of education... is not, as I think, to make them perfect in any one of the sciences, but so to open and dispose their minds, as may best make them capable of any, when they shall apply themselves to it. If men are, for a long time, accustomed to one sort or method of thoughts, their minds grow stiff in it, and do not readily turn to another. It is therefore to give them this freedom, that I think they should be made to look into all sorts of knowledge. But I do not propose it as a variety and stock of knowledge, but a variety and freedom of thinking; as an increase of the powers and activity of the mind, not an enlargement of its possessions."1 " We should always remember that the faculties of our souls are improved and made useful to us, just after the same manner as our bodies are.. Would you have a man write or paint, dance or fence well, or perform any other manual operation dextrously and with ease ? Let him have ever so much vigor and activity, suppleness and address naturally, yet nobody expects this from him unless he has been used to it, and has employed time and pains in fashioning and forming his hand, or outward parts, to these motions. Just so it is in the mind; would you have a man reason well, you must use him to it betimes, exercise his mind in observing the connection of ideas, and following them in

1 Bk. II, The Advancement of Learning.

2 The Interpretation of Nature.

1 Conduct of the Understanding, 19.

train. Nothing does this better than mathematics; which therefore I think should be taught all those who have the time and opportunity; not so much to make them mathematicians as to make them reasonable creatures." 1 Note that the question is begged here, for it is quite evident that one learns to fence only by practice in fencing and that that practice will not teach him to box or play tennis. Whereas Locke draws the conclusion that exercise in mathematical reasoning will make a man reason well, not only in mathematics but in all things. If we remember that the activities of mind " are improved and made useful to us just after the same manner as our bodies are," we will arrive at a conclusion very different from his. Locke himself goes back on his own theory, for in his " Thoughts on Education " (176) he writes: " I hear it is said that children should be employed in getting things by heart to exercise and improve their memories. I could wish this ware said with as much authority of reason as it is with forwardness of assurance, and that this practice were established upon good observation more than old custom. For it is evident that strength of memory is owing to a happy constitution and not to any habitual improvement got by exercise. Is it not the same with the other faculties ?"

1 Conduct of the Understanding, 6.

But every philosopher of that day wrote about the "faculties of the soul." Charles Bonnet (1720- 1793) even named his book " An Analytical Essay upon the Faculties of the Soul." Thomas Reed (1710-1796) wrote on "The Intellectual Powers of Man," and Condillac's (1715-1780) treatise was full of that doctrine. Nothing was more inevitable than that German Protestant schoolmasters when pressed for a reason for teaching the classics by their opponents, the philanthropists,|newly arrived champions of the practical studies, who succeeded indeed in discrediting the teaching of the old languages,| should have lighted upon this one and speedily made it the chief defense of their practice. In this way a doctrine persistently rejected for hundreds of years by the great teachers of mankind began to shape and preside over the educational practice of the western world. The theory upon which it is founded that the mind is divided into faculties is relatively very old, but the use of the doctrine in education is new, going back no farther than the eighteenth century.

When Friedrich August Wolf (1759-1824), the founder of the science of philology, began to go to school, he found that he could not bear a teacher more than three days together. Yet his precocity was so great that before he was two years old he knew a number of Latin words, and by the timehe was eight, could read an easy Latin author and had made a beginning of Greek and French. As long as his father taught him, all went well, but as soon as school-teachers began to instruct him, his troubles began. As long as he lived he was possessed by the conviction that he had been mistaught. He devoted his life to reforming the teaching of the classics. They had been studied as a preparatory qualification for the study of law and theology. To him this was the meanest view that could be taken of them. They are supposed to be the road to literature and learning. This is a traditional superstition, though there was a time when it was true. He proposes a different reason for studying them. They afford the "knowledge of human nature as exhibited in antiquity." 1

But Wolf's successors have not taught the classics for the reason that Wolf taught and believed in them. They have made of them an instrument for another purpose than that with which he sought to check the rise of the new-found realistic studies. They have resorted to " the grindstone theory" and not the knowledge theory to justify their use of them.

Is gymnastic training general or specific ? As we have seen, a warrant for this procedure is sought in the physical training of the gymnasium. Themind must be exercised as the body is. Its powers must be developed as the powers of the body are developed. This is surely a justification by confusion. Has the physical trainer any exercises that train the body as a whole? In the " Banquet" of Xenophon, Socrates is made to say that " those who have accustomed themselves to long foot races have thick legs and narrow shoulders, while on the contrary the wrestlers have broad shoulders and small legs. Now instead of producing such an effect, in the exercise of dancing, the feet, the legs, the neck, and indeed the whole body, are in action, and whoever would have his body supple, easy, and healthful, should learn to dance." Again, we find him saying in the " Memorabilia," " Do you not know that those who are by nature the weakest become, by exercising their bodies, stronger in those things in which they exercise them than those who neglect them, and bear the fatigue of exercise with greater ease ?" The physical trainer exercises special muscles and combinations of muscles. He has no single exercises which develop all forms of skill, nor has he any single exercises which will develop the single organs in more than particular ways. One man he teaches to box, another to row, another to work on the rings or the horse. But one who has learned boxing has not thereby learned to play tennis or to row. It may even be thatknowing how to perform one of these feats is a hindrance to learning another. The so-called general exercises are only selected groups of particular exercises, and train the special muscles involved in them to work together in the particular ways that they require. All-round athletes are rare, and the feats which an all-round athlete is expected to performl the pentathlon and the dekathlon I are by no means exhaustive tests of muscular ability. To anyone who goes in for this sort of thing it is quite apparent that physical education leads only to the acquirement of special forms of muscular skill. It is true that the exercising of any combination of muscles calls for a correspondingly rapid blood flow to build up the broken-down tissue. The blood must be more rapidly aerated, and quickened breathing is the result. These in some measure benefit the whole body if the exercises are taken in moderation, though they may greatly injure the heart or the digestive and secretory systems if they are not. If any part of the brain is specially engaged in mental work, it would seem possible that a correspondingly rapid blood supply is distributed to that organ. Just what the details of the effects of physical training are is by no means clear, as the subject is exceedingly intricate and demands much more attention than has yet been given it. This much seems to beplain, that there is really no such thing as general strength of body or even of any one of the organs of the body. Strength varies in proportion to habit- uation of muscles in working together to perform the different feats of skill. If one is to be a pianist or a surgeon, it is conceivable that he should not engage in perfecting the work of his larger muscles, as they might get in his way and become not contributory but rival forms of skill, as walking is to an adult who tries to learn to swim. Physical skill is specific, and its variations are the more or less of specific activities. What we call general physical training is training in several specific forms of activity, and only by a figure of speech is it all-round training.

1 See Mark Pattison, Essay on F. A. Wolf.

Are there any faculties of the mind? Let us look now at the faculties of the mind and inquire concerning the possibility of training or developing *the* judgment, *the* will, *the* imagination, *the* observation, or *the* memory, each in general, that is, formally. Taking the last one first because the facts in regard to it are matters of everyday knowledge, we must first note that the psychologists tell us there is no such thing as a single organ or faculty of memory which can be trained as a whole. We have a different memory for everything we remember. Familiar experience tells the same thing. Some of us remember faces but not names, and someremember names but not faces; some the names of books, but not their contents, others the contents and not the names; some remember the words of foreign languages, but others forget them as soon as learned. We know that we do not remember all things equally well, that our memories insist upon being partial and particular. We see the same thing in other people. I used to go from San Francisco to Berkeley daily on " the racing boat," the ferry boat which took the crowds that followed the races over to the track. My neighbors were interesting folk, for they represented a high degree of specialization in education. They were people with marvelous memories for the names, the pedigrees, the performances, and the selling prices of running horses. They seemed to recall all there was to be recalled about jockeys, weights, conditions of the track, etc. Their going-and-coming conversation was so thickly charged with facts of that sort as to put to shame the sievelike memory of a poor student which at times seemed to refuse to hold anything at all. But suppose these same people, with their marvelously developed memories, had been thrust into a theological school and required to commit St. John's Gospel, the deeds of the saints, and the hymns of the Church, would they have succeeded any better than the rest of us ? Yet their memories were highly trained.

There were two students in the University of California who set out to train their memories by committing the whole of Milton's " Paradise Lost," and one recent student at Cambridge, England, is said to have committed the whole of the Iliad. Do / men who do these things remember the calculus, organic chemistry, or the facts in Blackstone's " Commentaries " better because of forcing themselves in this fashion? John Locke thought not, Cardinal Newman thought not and spoke of having known men "who could without effort run through the succession of days on which Easter fell for years back; or could say where they were, or what they were doing, on a given day in a given year; or could recollect the Christian names of friends and strangers; or could enumerate in exact order the names of all the shops from Hyde Park corner to the Bank; or had so mastered the University Calendar as to be able to bear an examination in the academical history of any M.A., taken at random. And I believe in most of these cases the talent, in its exceptional character, did not extend beyond several classes of subjects. There are a hundred memories as there are a hundred virtues." 1 Pathological cases have shown that the memory of one sense may be lost without that of the others being impaired. Professor James determined to test the matter. He first committed 158 lines of Victor Hugo's " Satyr." It took some part of eight days and a total time of 13if minutes. He then trained his memory by working twenty minutes a day in committing " Paradise Lost," and finally committed the first book. He then went back to Victor Hugo's "Satyr" and found that to commit 158 additional lines 151- minutes were required, or twenty minutes more than before training his memory by committing the " Paradise Lost." He admits that during the second test he was fatigued by other work. But four of his students repeated the test. Two of them showed considerable gain after practice, and two none at all. Professor James stated it as his conviction that the native retentiveness which we bring with us at birth cannot be changed. "All improvement of the memory lies in the line of *elaborating the associates* of each of the several kinds of things to be remembered. No amount of culture would seem capable of modifying a man's general retentiveness."1 Every so-called method of training the memory is simply a method of studying the facts to be remembered I a better method of going to work to associate them with other facts etc. " When schoolboys improve by practice in ease of learning by heart, the improvement will, I am sure, be always found to reside in the *mode of study*

1 Richardson, The Choice of Books, p. 79. New York, 1905.

1 James, Psychology, Briefer Course, pp. 296-298. New York, 1900.

of the particular piece (due to the greater interest, the greater suggestiveness, the generic similarity with other pieces, the more sustained attention, etc.), and not at all to any enhancement of the brute retentive power." 1 This distinction helps us materially to locate the kind of discipline of the memory which is impossible and tells us definitely what we should attempt to do instead. We are to let *the memory* alone and to bend our energies to the proper comprehension of facts which are worth remembering. It is the content and not the form of memory which is to be trained.

Can the memory be trained? Now come the critics of Professor James's view who, though their investigations have not materially changed his results, have sometimes talked and written of them as though they had and, by so doing, have brought confusion instead of clearness and lent an unwarranted degree of comfort to the enemy. In 1905 Ebert and Meumann published the results of elaborate and seemingly thoroughgoing tests of eight subjects who were first measured by being required to commit a miscellaneous assortment of letters, numbers, nonsense syllables, words, Italian words, strophes of poetry, and bits of prose. Next they undertook to determine which methods of learning were most economical. In the investigation theylearned thirty-two series of nonsense syllables, ordinarily learning two series of syllables on one day and testing the retention of two more. This went on for sixteen days, at the end of which time the arst material was relearned and the results before and after training were compared. Four of the subjects went through a further period of training by means of sixteen additional series and the original condition was then again compared. The tables show that there was a gain in each case. " The results," says Professor Pillsbury, " fell out entirely in favor of the view that special training gives a general effect."1 Professor Dearborn, who repeated Meumann's experiments with great care, found no evidence of general memory training in his results. Professor Pillsbury also quotes the experiments of Winch on school children in Great Britain, in which about one hundred children learned selections from a historical reader and were then divided into two groups, one group being trained for four mornings by committing about one hundred words of poetry, while the members of the other did sums. On the fifth morning each group committed a second test passage, and it was found that the members of the group which had been trained did this on the average about ten per cent better than those who had worked the sums. But what do these testsshow? Do they not show improvement in memorizing a particular kind of material by learning a particular method of study and increasing one's interest in doing a particular kind of thing, rather than improvement of *the memory in general"*. The percentage of gain reported by Meumann in the third test over the first is 59 in the case of numbers, 42 in the case of nonsense syllables, and only 29 in the case of prose words. This does not seem to mean that " general strength " of memory has been developed, but rather that several particular interests have been improved markedly, and independently, by training. If " general strength " is developed by training a given faculty or function, have we not a right to demand that that " strength " shall be general, that is, available in nearly equal measure for all related kinds of use ? All the experiments show that it is not, and in them all we have what seems very much more like a readaptation of a method than the repetitive functioning of a developed organ. Again, what are claimed as general results are of so little value that, even if they were clearly made out, education could not consider them as of any importance whatever, and certainly would not be warranted in shaping its work to get them. The results seem to confirm Professor James's view that all so-called improvement of the memory is improvement in method of studying.Dr. Fracker found that practice in committing the order of four tones led to improvement in the committing of poetry. So did committing the order of presentation of four shades of gray, of nine shades of gray, of nine geometrical figures, of nine numbers, and of the extent of arm movements. His conclusion is that his results accord with those of Professor James, " inasmuch as all the factors we have discovered have to do with methods," that is, with ways of learning that are specific and common to both the test and the practice operations.

1 James, Psychology, Briefer Course, pp. 296-298.

1 Latin and Greek in American Education, p. 367. New York, 1911.

The question of the transferability of training is not the question of formal discipline. The question as to whether or not a method of study or mental action learned in one context can be applied to a recognizably similar problem is not the question of formal discipline. The mind is a generalizes We are never called upon to apply what we have learned to just the same conditions as those in which we learned it. If the method called for is the same and the context in which it was learned is sufficiently like the context which presents the problem to call it forth, there will undoubtedly be a transferring of what was learned in the old situation to what is required in the new. The whole theory of habit supports this view. We tend to repeat the motions we have already learned, whenever the situation is not too confusing to allow usto do so; but let the situation be very novel, and even our most deep-seated habits refuse to function well in it. I can walk a ten-inch plank with ease on the ground; but let it be put fifty feet in the air, and I find it nearly impossible to walk along it. Undoubtedly much is transferred from my practice of walking on the ground to the new situation in which I find myself compelled to walk high in air; but he would indeed be a foolish thinker who would maintain that the art of walking is one and of such a kind that, having once learned it, one can walk anywhere. While there are common elements in all walking, they do not of themselves help me to walk along a wire. To master that situation I must be specifically trained for that kind of walking. It is the same with talking. It is one thing to talk well in the bosom of one's family, and quite another to talk well in the presence of strangers, and still a third thing to talk well in making a public speech. And so different are these arts that few orators have been conversationalists and few conversationalists orators.

The numerous psychological experiments which have attempted to determine the limits within which what is learned in one context can be applied to another are valuable as showing the conditions under which the mind functions as a generalizer. But have not the men who reportedthem confused two questions which ought to be kept clearly separated I the first, Is there such a thing as a general, or wholesale, training of the faculties or functions of the mind ? and the second, To what extent is what is learned in one context applied in a similar one ? The first question is answered not by finding out to what extent generalization goes on, but by finding out whether it can go on at all without faculties and without common contexts to call it forth. In other words, the acceptance of the fundamental doctrine of modern psychology, that there are no faculties in the mind, of itself necessitated the abandonment of the doctrine of formal training in education. The coming of the day when no teacher uses this hoary superstition to justify his teaching has actually been postponed by experiments undertaken to show to what extent a common element may function in different fields of learning.

Is judgment one? It is hardly necessary to apply a similar criticism to the training of each of the so-called faculties. If judgment were one, it could perhaps be trained as one. But men who think equally well upon all kinds of subjects are not to be found. " It is said," writes Professor Angell, " that education ought to train one's ability to execute analyses, to make accurate inferences, and to detect essential relations, as though analyses and inferences and relations were names for perfectly homogeneous, uniform processes. The futility of this conception in the form in which it is often advocated requires no psychology more recondite than that afforded by common observation and a very modest type of common sense. If the world were built in a neat snug-fitting box, with all parts interchangeable, the scheme ought to work admirably. Unhappily the type of analysis and inference which is valid in mathematics, for instance, is practically very different from that which is valid in linguistics and history. A similar discontinuity of inferential procedure marks off from one another sundry other fields of knowledge. Surely from this side the most that educational doctrine can ask or urge is that the mind shall be brought into contact with all of the great characteristic divisions of human thought and that the processes in each of these domains shall be made familiar. . . . Psychologically, of course, the various forms of reasoning process reduce to one or two simple types with their variants. But practically the content of the ideas with which thought has to deal is often so diverse as to render discipline gained on this score in one direction of only the most remote consequence in another." 1 Reasoning, then, is a specific rather than a general activity.

1 Pillsbury,LatinandGreekinAmericanEducation,p.357. NewYork,1911.

Is there a faculty of observation or of imagination ? The observation is another faculty which we are urged to train, but good observation seems always to be a function of the particular content that one has been habituated to observe. Take three trained observers out to observe the same landscape. Let one be a real-estate dealer, one a railroad-constructing engineer, and one a landscape artist. Can they possibly see the same things in the landscape ? Yet each is a trained observer. One sees with the ideas which are in his mind, with his apperceptive system, and it is only by developing that that his eyes can learn to see what they should see.

Imagination also cannot be trained as one. It too is a function of the content. First, it is divided into rather well-marked types, which are by no means interchangeable, so that a person of a markedly audile type is hardly warranted in attempting to substitute another type by training. Then within each type we have a different imagination for each thing that we image. Here again the counsel of psychology to education would seem to be to let *the* imagination alone and put its efforts upon securing clear pictures of those matters and concerns which should be clearly registered in the mind.

It is the same with attention. It is primarily selective. We attend to those things which interest us, which are problems for us, which belong to the line of goods we carry. It is, in each of us, not one but many, and always the result not of an abstract but of a series of concrete developments. To quote Professor Angell again: " So far as these several forms of attention have divergent elements in them (and certainly there are many such divergences both of sensory content and of motor attitude) we shall hardly be entitled to look for beneficial effects in the use of one form of attention as a result of discipline in another form of it." And so with all the other mental and moral virtues. They are not general but obstinately particular. What, then, is the net result of all this? What but that we must abandon all talk and claim of general mind-forming, and gladly accept the more humble task of mind- informing. The several studies provide not opportunities for general training, but each of them its own peculiar opportunities for special training. The opposite of formal training is content training. Each study offers its content of facts profitable to be known, and its content of methods of dealing with those facts. But both its methods and its facts belong to its content and are valuable only when taken together. We may teach them broadly or we may teach them narrowly, and, unless our pupils are inventive geniuses of the rare sort, they will not get from our teaching much more than we invitethem to get. To my mind the most suggestive of all the experiments upon this subject which have been reported is the modest effort of Professor Bagley, which showed that the children who were instructed to hand in neat arithmetic papers did so, but did not improve their geography and language papers a bit. But when Professor Ruediger enlarged the lesson and took pains to impress upon similar children the need for neatness in preparing all their papers, neatness began to characterize them all. Must we not teach concretely what we would have our students learn, and abandon all confidence in the mystical power of studies?

4

SECTION 4

CHAPTER IV
EDUCATION AS WORLD BUILDING

Our worlds are different. The world of the man who is born blind must be strikingly different from the world of the person who sees. The same landscape stretches before him that stretches before us, but he lacks something. Other folks experience the infinitely varied play of light and shade, but he cannot know them nor objects as defined by them. Others cannot by verbal descriptions, even the most perfect, impart their experience to him. How it feels to see he can never know, and how one gets along without the aid of visual images with which to define a world of things will be an incomprehensible mystery to us as long as we have them. The world of the deaf must be a queer, still world, which we who love the sound of voices and of music cannot know. The deaf and the blind make their world out of another sort of stuff than that which we build into ours. Yet when we think of it they are but striking cases of a common law. All our experiences are private and particular. My see- ings, hearings, touchings, tastings, smellings, are my own; the ether vibrations which stimulate themin me have not reached your retina; the sound waves which fall upon my ear have not broken upon your tympanum. Your seeings and hearings are yours; mine are mine. Though we do have similar senses we do not have the same sense material, and the worlds which we construct from it differ accordingly. It is a commonplace that the soldier's world is different from the sailor's, the farmer's from the lawyer's, the Eskimo's from that of the dweller in the tropics, the Chinaman's from the American's, the youth's from the man's, the child's from the adult's. The experience stuff with which each one builds is peculiar to himself, and the scheme of things which each of us carries about with him is different from the scheme of things which every other man possesses.

Our feelings are not transferable. My world may have points of identity with other people's worlds. How thoroughgoingly we view matters in the same way is nevertheless very hard for us to tell. We are each of us shut off by ourselves. Our feelings are not interchangeable; there is no process of telepathy by which you can pass your weariness, or hunger, or suffering, or conviction, or joy to me. In this horrible year (1915) when more individuals are in agony than ever before in the history of men one sometimes wakes with a start of astonishment that his own body does not quiver with pain from their gunshot wounds or their gnawing hunger. It is true their suffering makes us suffer, but our suffering is not of like kind with theirs. When they are struck down we do not feel the flash of agony that shoots through them.

This relentless privacy of experience in which we are shut up forces us to struggle desperately to make our inner being known. But all our efforts at direct communication are unavailing. I can never be sure when you say the stone is hard or the toothache hurts that you have quite the same kind of feeling when you strike the stone or suffer from the toothache that I have. I can never sample your pain and match it with my own. I can only watch your acts and from them reason I if I acted so it would be because I felt thus. If my nearest friend tells me that he believes in a certain course of action, I can only watch to see what he does to find out if his belief is real. If he avows that he is convinced by the proof which I show him, I must wait to see how he acts before I can be sure whether he is or no. The evidence that we have experience in common is always indirect, is our community of action. Oneness of thought does hot manifest itself in any other way. We may agree in words, yet there would be a marked decrease in the number of lawsuits which are brought to trial if our minds had actually united in the understandings concerning which they were in nominal accord. One can hardly have lived through the events of the last year without having had his faith in community of human intentions when evidenced by a common language wrested away. Speech is a very inexact revealer of our feelings, convictions, and purposes. Our words go out; our thoughts remain with us.

Our common world a social construct. We talk about the world as though it were an existence which had revealed itself in the same way and almost to the same extent to each one of us. Yet our personal experiences of it are various, fragmentary, confusing, and fall far short of that oneness of objectivity to which our words seem to refer. Two persons who look at the same object, or listen to the same music, or read the same book, do not have the same experience of them though they may talk as though they had. Each one takes the matter as it appears to him and attaches to it the significance or meaning which his past experiences enable him to supply. " No two persons have quite the same experience even of a rosebud," says Professor Lloyd Morgan in his lectures on "The Interpretation of Nature." We do not start with one fixed world of objects which each of us finds ready-made and mirrors perfectly, carrying about thereafter a little film or image of it in his mind, the same kind of an offprint of it which hisneighbor has. Knowledge-getting is not a process of copying. It is a process of constructing. The consternation-making fact is that we do not start with a common world of things, the perfect mirroring of which by our minds would make each of us know one and the same world. We start with see- ings, hearings, touchings, tastings, smellings, which are peculiarly our own, dissimilar to those of others to a degree, wholly nontransferable; and out of this manyness of feeling we proceed to construct common centers of reference, and cooperative ways of procedure which we name by common names and come to regard as demanding of us a more or less common and established system of reactions. Our own experiences have a reality which is immediate and compelling. Other people's experiences exist for us only in so far as we can put ourselves in their places, interpreting their acts in terms of our own feelings. The world which we speak of as common to us all is a social construct, the world of our discourse, of our common action, a unity of operation. It is a part of the world which our own private feelings tell us about, but they tell of much more than it. We start with diversified experiences and work toward the identities of objects mutually understood, not from the unity of one and the same set of objects to the diversity of conflicting individual interpretations of them.

Mechanical education due to a false philosophy. Nothing can be more devastating to the work of education than false notions of what the process of knowledge-getting is. Most teachers assume that the universe of ready-made objects is given, that we must start from it. Knowledge-getting consists in allowing such parts of it as we want to know to impress themselves upon the receptive mind. " Here is the world," they say, " look at it"; or "Here is wisdom I learn to repeat its words." The whole dreary soul-destroying business of mechanical education, which has existed century after century and in most of the schools of every country of the world, is due to this mistaken philosophy of knowledge. We are active beings, it conceives us as passive; we are made to see with our own eyes and hear with our own ears and understand and construct with our own understandings, but this philosophy of education robs us of our birthright by hindering us from using our own senses in gathering experiences and our own minds in constructing these sense feelings into a self-made world, for it attempts to substitute for these natural and meaningful experiences of the self, familiarity with the words of other men.

How does the child make his world? Let us go back to the child and ask him how he builds his world. He is born, as each one of us was, withthat mysterious power of awareness which tells us all that we know or ever shall know about the existence of anything. All that we say is or is not has revealed its existence or its nonexistence to men through this medium. Whatever we talk about, think about, hope, fear, and expect, whether it belongs to the past, to the present, or the future, comes to us in this guise. To say that a thing I anything I is is merely to employ a shortened form of expression for the thought that someone is aware of it, that it has revealed its being to some mind.

The child, we say, brings into the world with him this marvelous potency of having experiences and a nervous system with its complement of sense organs, eyes, ears, organs of touch and smell, and nerve endings for tasting. He is born among men who have been living a long time and who have learned to distinguish the various kinds of feelings which they have had, to separate hard from soft, harmful from helpful, safe from dangerous, to draw a thousand other lines of division between the parts of their awareness, to combine these parts into clusters of feelings and to project them into a world of ordered things, and thereupon, by using the feeling of a single sense as the evidence of associated feelings which have been grouped with it, they have learned to order their anticipations accordingly. He is born with the same potency to have experiences that they started with; he must learn to make distinctions in the same way that they did. He must experiment for himself and out of his own experience build up his own notions of things. Their greater knowledge enables them in some degree to select experiences for him, that is, to put him in the way of having them; but their experience will not stand proxy for his any more than their health releases him from the necessity of maintaining his own. If we were scrupulously careful we would not, I think, say of this child that he must learn to live *in the world;* we would say instead that he must learn to live the world.

Of all this as yet he knows nothing. If we place a lighted candle in front of him, put a bitter substance in his mouth, or make a loud sound near him, he will not seem to note them, for when newborn he responds but feebly to all kinds of stimuli. The feelings which we call smell, taste, touch, hearing, and sight, and which to us are the signs of things, seem in him to be quite dull and vague at first. His lips and tongue are the most sensitive parts of his body. He is quite helpless to keep his arms from moving and utterly unable to control his muscles. But by the twenty-third day Preyer's son followed a moving candle with his eyes and turned his head in order to do so. The organism now begins to be mature enough to start upon that seemingly most exciting of all careers, the reaching for what one sees, the tasting of what one touches, and the tearing and flinging about of all that one's hands fall upon that the mouth refuses. The senses now are wide-awake. There is endless agitation of eyes, hands, and mouth in carrying on their awkward sampling of surroundings. What a curious jumbled awareness must that be of which they are the bodily counterpart! Professor James has described it as " one big blooming buzzing confusion." " That confusion," he declares, " is the baby's universe; and the universe of all of us is still to a great extent such a confusion, potentially resolvable, and demanding to be resolved, but not yet actually resolved into parts." The process of learning, therefore, which we each begin at birth and are bound to continue until we die is a process of bringing order out of the chaos of our own confused impressions, of noting distinctions in feelings which at first were only vague and indeterminate, and of systematizing these reports of feeling into a world of articulated things. We always start with a vague experience, and out of it step by step we carve the parts which need demands | an order of procedure just the opposite of that process of beginning with clear-cut things and elementary parts and putting them together into wholes which education is commonly conceived to be.

He must make his notions of all that exists. The child does not start with things which he finds ready-made and has only to look upon and mentally photograph; things of that well-defined sort exist only for adult minds and are the results, not the beginnings, of a long process of experience. The things of our world are unknown to him. He has to begin at the beginning and make his notions of all that exists. You and I know that the candle flame will burn us if we touch it. He has to burn his finger to find out what sort of a thing it is. Hold up an orange before him. It is the first time that he has ever seen one. What will an orange be to him ? He will be aware of yellow, though he will not know it by that name or distinguish it clearly from other experiences of color. The outline he will hardly get. To be aware of its shape, weight, and texture he must take it in his hand. He cannot have a feeling of its taste until he bites into it. He is so set up when he comes into the world that he binds together the reports of these different senses and makes one thing out of them. Henceforth the look of the orange will suggest the taste, the shape, the weight, and the texture which he has found can be gotten from a thing with that sort of a look.

Language not a substitute for experience. There are two points to be noted: first, the thing whichever after he will know as an orange he has built up out of his own several kinds of experience of it I no amount of verbal description of it could possibly have given him this knowledge. Language cannot impart experiences; that, perhaps, is the reason why we do not name things. But language can call up within us experiences which we have already had and can help us to understand their meaning and organize them in such ways as to anticipate coming experiences and so control them. Language is all conceptual, and concepts as we have seen are not existences but workings which we perform upon existences. " Percepts without concepts are blind, and concepts without percepts are empty." Facts, information, and information studies are useless because we have learned to do nothing with them. They report what once existed but is now dead. The knowledge of them does not help us to get ready for anything like them which we must expect will come again and must get ready for. But principles, laws, kinds, are recurring experiences, and knowledge of them will help us to get ready to handle instances of them when they arise.

The second point is that if language cannot give us experiences but can only help us to work with or interpret those we already have, we must each of us go on building up our notions of the particularthings which make up our world as long as we live in just the same way that the child builds up his notion of the orange. Sense experience gives us the only knowledge which we have of individual things. To know them we must handle them, turn them over, pull them to pieces, and work with them, as well as look at them. If we once get this experience of them, we can apply it to everything else of that kind, but without it our knowledge of kinds is only empty words. Language enables us to work with experiences I it is not a substitute for them. No one can make either percepts or concepts for another person. Each of us must work them out for himself. But others can aid us immensely by putting us in the way of doing that and by challenging us. to do it. The necessities and the opportunities with which they surround us in order that we may learn to use our own minds must provide opportunities for both perceptual and conceptual experience and construction on our part I opportunities both for learning the nature of concrete things at first hand and for organizing our experience of them by classifying them into kinds, and working out summary statements, principles, rules or laws concerning their behavior. Object lessons in which the student makes the acquaintance of real things either in the classroom or by means of excursions, workshops, laboratories, practicework, or investigations privately undertaken are as indispensable a feature of education as the lessons which assume a concrete knowledge of a subject and proceed to help the student to systematically conceptualize the percepts which he already has.

The world outside and the world inside. It is interesting, I think, to go back for a moment to the child and to ask him for some further details of the process by which he builds his world. In the first place we must repeat that all that either he or anyone else ever knows about himself or about anything else is by means of his awareness. Nothing exists either for him or for anyone except as it reveals itself in his consciousness. It is not things but things experienced that make up our world. Is the grass green, the apple sour, the rose red, the night dark each to itself? Before there can be any color there must be an eye upon whose retina ether waves are vibrating at rates of from 392,00x3,000,000 to 757,000,000,000 per second. The lower are the red rays, the upper the violet rays, of the spectrum. But these rays do not penetrate to the brain; they stop at the retina. To it they communicate some kind of change, and this in turn it communicates to the brain and produces a feeling which we call seeing. Air waves vibrating at rates of from 16 to 40,000 per second break upon the tympanum and communicate their motion to thefluids of the auditory canal. They do not penetrate to the brain, but the changes in our feeling which ensue we call hearing. The sense of touch too provides its quota of feelings of a peculiar quality. It begins to be active almost as soon as the eye is, and like the eye each of these senses produces at first but vague, suffused, and nonlocalized feelings.

Awareness as yet is not separated into two parts | awareness of self and awareness of things. The world which begins as a blur must be dichotomized into internal and external, subjective and objective. This distinction is introduced within experience by a slow and never completely effective process. The instincts" which the child brings with him make his eyes partial to moving things. The hand is a moving thing; the eye follows it in its explorative movements and sees it as it touches the object. They learn to work together. Touchings and see- ings now are related. This leads to an expectation that when one of them is experienced the other will be. The look of things can now make us aware of their hardness or softness, their weight, shape, size, and probable distance from us.

But when one touches any part of his body the feeling is very unlike that which attends the touching of things which are not his own body. When one's hand touches his body the hand reports a feeling of touching and the body one of beingtouched. These are called the feelings of active and of passive touch. The eye of the child sees the hand touch the object and at the same time feels the touch; but when the eye sees it touching the body the hand feels what it touches and what is touched also feels that it is being touched. Henceforth whatever feels the hand when it touches belongs to myself, and whatever does not is different. Thus the vague of feeling is split in two | into internal, or my own body's feelings, and external, or things experienced without letting me know in the same way that they are being experienced. In this way our awareness begins to be divided into two great irreconcilable hemispheres which no matter how far we incline to thrust them apart are but distinctions introduced within our total awareness.

Each sense furnishes material for construction. The other sense feelings are in the conspiracy from the first. If we but stop to count out all the things which our world would not contain had we been born stone deaf, we begin to appreciate how large a part of it we make out of the feelings which we call our experience of sound. Smell also provides material for construction into things. Mr. Bradley conceives it to be the sense which supplies experiences of reality to the dog; so that, he thinks, the dog's logic can be written in one sentence" What smells is real, what does not smell is nothing." Itwould seem that these feelings have a diminishing usefulness to man, though it is quite unlikely that he will ever be able to get along without them. The poet who wrote

Smells are surer than sounds or sights
To make your heartstrings crack.
They start those awful voices o' nights
That whisper, " Old man, come back."

refers to a fact in us which is as deep-seated even as our animal nature. We make a peculiarly vital part of our world out of these feelings, and their recurrences recall to us the most poignant and penetrating of experiences. That taste also supplies bricks for our world building is shown by the fact that this word has become a general designation for experiences which are acceptable and which when it is coupled with the adjective *bad* are regarded as unfit for human use.

Our experiences of temperature furnish us a basis for dividing the earth into zones and for determining the desirability of its parts for human habitation. They also shape our very anticipations of the future world. Our philosophies of conduct and our schemes of punishment and reward we construct in terms of pleasure and pain. If our nature were different how different a world we would know! With other sense organs we should have a different universe.

We arrange our experiences in a temporal and spatial order. Time and space we seem simply to find, not at all to make. Yet if awareness lasted but for an instant, and each instant then passed utterly away so that no trace of it remained, and a completely new instant took its place, would there be any such thing as time ? If our minds were like a camera in which one plate is exposed for a moment and shut off, and a new plate is then exposed, would there be any experience of time ? Is there any such thing as time for the camera plates ? My clock is ticking on the mantelpiece. I call it a timekeeper. Does it really keep time? Every tick vanishes before the next one begins. It must be that they do not know each other, that it is I who keep the tick that has gone, and the one that is going, and the one that is coming, and the one that will follow it, in mind. It is I who hold the parts of the series together and make them a series, just as I hold the tones of the instruments together and make music possible. Without this remembering of the past after it is past, and this relating of it to the present and of both of these to the future, there would be no such a thing as the time we know.

It is one thing to have this peculiar kind of awareness and quite another to employ it in constructing an elaborate time-ordered world. Menexperienced time perhaps for what we now call hundreds of thousands of years before they arranged events by time tables, or had a care to discriminate the seasons or retain the order of the years. Even the eager-minded Greeks do not seem to have had much success in constructing a calendar, and the greatest historian of antiquity, Thucyd- ides "avoided dates as far as he could, and made his years consist merely of a long summer and a short winter." 1 If it were possible to look into the minds of men to see what kind of a world they have constructed for themselves, it is likely that in no respect would such shocking diversity be found to obtain as in their arranging of experiences in time. Beyond a narrow immediate present to which we relate the recent past and the close coming future, events of which we are aware do not tend to organize themselves in a well-outlined time series. The work of making a world whose past is articulate calls for a difficult constructive effort which the student himself must undertake. He must make his own organization of history or suffer the penalty of living in a world with very narrow horizons and of confused and disorderly happenings.

1 See the very interesting article on "The Discovery of Time," by James T. Shotwell in *The Journal of Philosophy, Psychology, and Scientific Methods,* under date of April 15, 1915.

It is not otherwise with space. If we are constrained to think of it as something we see and do not construct, let us ask what our experience of space would be if the horizon-bounded picture which spreads before us whenever we look out upon the world were to disappear utterly from consciousness as soon as we turned away from it to look at another object; if through life one visual picture succeeded another, but always the first one completely passed away so that we never knew but one. Would such a notion of space as we now have be possible then? Do not our minds make it by putting beside the visual field of our perception the visual field of our memories and on the other side the visual field of our anticipation? And is it not necessary for the child to build up his notion of a space world by persistent efforts of the same sort as he must employ in making for himself a world whose parts are arranged according to a time order ? In all of this we must remember that no matter what things are about him, nor what historical facts have preceded him, nor how widely the universe stretches out before the gaze of those who have already constructed a well-ordered image of it, that none of these things will avail him at all until he himself can experience them. Education concerns itself not with things but with our experiences of things. If in any single case the learnerfails to experience the thing which it sets before him as needful for him to know, the instruction has invso far been a failure.

How persons are distinguished from things. As yet we have said nothing of the world of persons, but have been calling all the groupings which his feeling enables the child to make " things." It is time to make a distinction, a distinction which even little children are led by their feelings to begin to make as soon as they are two or three months old. Something different goes on inside the small child when a stranger comes into the room and takes him in his arms from what goes on when his mother or nurse handles him, and something very different goes on inside him when his mother or nurse comes into the room and takes him in her arms from that which went on before when no person was in the room and the cradle was holding him. The smallest infant but a few days old gives clear evidence of having one awareness for persons and another awareness for things. Its feeling of hunger gives place to contentment, of chill to warmth, of fixity in one position to the relief of changed positions, when mother or nurse comes in. A social sense may not be necessary to explain its awareness of persons; if it exists it would but help the other changes in its feelings to group themselves about their cause. This first stage, inwhich awareness is more aware of persons than of surrounding things, Professor Baldwin has called " the projective stage in the growth of the child's personal consciousness." In its cradle the baby watches its mother and singles out her goings and comings for special attention. Little by little he is getting control of his muscles and teaching his hands and mouth, and eyes and hands, and finally his eyes and legs to work together. What is so natural as that he should continue this process by making his hands, his face, and finally his legs repeat or imitate the movements that he sees; and so when the ministering body smiles at him he smiles back, when she waves her hand he tries to do so, too. Finally he begins to imitate the copy by standing erect and walking. But all these new acts bring new stresses and strains, and each involves new feelings which are particularly vivid when he thus tries to perform a new act.

How he makes the notion of self. This purposive striving makes him aware of himself, and thus we reach the subjective stage in the growth of the self-notion. But the feeling of waving my hands, of trying to make sounds like the sounds I hear, of walking like other folks, which lead me first to know myself, must be like the feeling which that other body has when it waves its hands, makes the sounds which I try to make, and walks as I try towalk. So " the *subjective* becomes *ejective*; that is, other people's bodies, says the child to himself, have experiences *in them* such as mine has. . . . The ' ego' and the ' alter' are thus born together. Both are crude and unreflective, largely organic, and the two get purified and clarified together by this twofold reaction between project and subject and between subject and eject. My sense of myself grows by imitation of you, and my sense of yourself grows in terms of my sense of myself."
1

We make ourselves in the image of our environment. The truly remarkable thing is the thoroughness with which we make ourselves out of the experiences which we have of the people around us. Young cocks, it is said, do not learn to crow, or young dogs to bark well, or young canary birds to sing well, if they are prevented from hearing their elders perform these feats. And so very plastic is the young child that, in the very few cases in which he has been brought up by animals, it is said that he became an animal, going on four feet, eating raw meat, and clawing and tearing his way through life, much as his foster parents had done while he was among them. Be this as it may, Plato, Aristotle, and Quintilian were quite justified in believing that speech is shaped and character largelyformed in the earliest years, and upon the model which mother or nurse provides. And Freud and Jung seem amply warranted in believing that it is the experiences of our earliest years that give the character a permanent bent throughout life. At any rate, though we continue to make ourselves in the image of the persons with whom we are familiar, and to return the compliment by making them in our image as long as we live, this is the period in which we go about it most vigorously, the period when it comes nearest being the sole business of life. After these years we tend to put our capital to work to buy and sell experiences with it, and later on to live on the interest which it brings.

1 Baldwin, Social and Ethical Interpretations in Mental Development, p. 15. New York, 1906.

The struggle with institutions for existence. The child then is born into a world of persons, and sent into life so made up that he constructs his acts and, consequently, his feelings upon the models which they furnish him. But not only does he inherit the racial instincts of the human family; he inherits also the racial environment which his forbears have been preparing for thousands, perhaps even for millions, of years before his coming. Was it not Napoleon who said, " It is not man who lives, but institutions " ? At any rate, it is not true; for it is only men that live, though they may indeed allow the dead hand of their ancestors to shapetheir lives for them to the extent of becoming mere phantoms of the past. Thus life is not only a struggle for food, clothing, and shelter, but a never-ending struggle to determine whether men themselves shall live or institutions shall live for them.

One of the chiefest of these institutions is language. The child is caught up into its network of ready-made distinctions and racially established meanings almost before he leaves his cradle. Up to this time he has been busily engaged in making his world out of his own feelings. Now he perforce becomes a nominalist and is invited to name things instead of experiencing them. Thus language tends to substitute ready-made sounds for felt experiences, knowledge about things for knowledge of them. It turns us over to a world of hard- and-fast things which are not to us meanings, but every one of which has been constructed by our ancestors out of their feelings in just the same way that the child has thus far constructed so much of a world as he has succeeded in making. But language opens to him a new world of meanings, we say; it helps to make thought definite. Yes, that is true, but there is grave danger in it also. The child who is..merely told about things cannot be said to experience them; he is not getting the race's knowledge of them. Indeed, "because conceptswithout percepts are empty," he is being kept from a knowledge of them. This process becomes the more destructive when the relatively imperishable memory of written and printed books prevents the normal death of tradition. By their means definitions are kept alive, meanings have force, and conventions and traditions rule long after the occasion for their existence has disappeared. It is thus that the letter killeth and only the spirit which makes the letter is alive. Recall that remarkable story which Plato tells in the "Phaedrus." It contains a warning. " At the Egyptian city of Naucratis, there was a famous old god whose name was Theuth; the bird which is called the Ibis is sacred to him, and he was the inventor of many arts, such as arithmetic and calculation and geometry and astronomy and draughts and dice, but his great discovery was the use of letters. Now in those days the god Thamus was the king of the whole country of Egypt; and he dwelt in that great city of upper Egypt which the Hellenes call Egyptian Thebes, and the god himself is called by them Ammon. To him came Theuth and showed his inventions, desiring that the other Egyptians might have the benefit of them; he enumerated them and Thamus inquired about their several uses, and praised some of them and censured others, as he approved or disapproved ofthem. It would take a long time to repeat all that Thamus said to Theuth in praise or blame of the various arts. But when they came to letters, This, said Theuth, will make the Egyptians wiser and give them better memories; it is a specific both for the memory and for the wit. Thamus replied, O most ingenious Theuth, the parent or inventor of an art is not always the best judge of the utility or inutility of his own inventions to the users of them. And in this instance you, who are the father of letters, from a paternal love of your own children have been led to attribute to them a quality which they cannot have; for this discovery of yours will create forgetfulness in the learners' souls, because they will not use their memories; they will trust to the external written characters and not remember of themselves. The specific which you have discovered is an aid not to memory, but to reminiscence, and you give your disciples not truth, but only the semblance of truth; they will be hearers of many things and will have learned nothing; they will be a tiresome company, having the show of wisdom without the reality." 1

The function of language. Now, whatever education may do, it must provide the reality of wisdom, not its husk merely. It must recognize the fact that knowledge of the word is not knowledgeof the thing, and that to know the word is a matter quite other than to experience its meaning. Neither spoken nor written language can convey perceptions or thought, and neither in conversation, speeches, lectures, nor books do we impart them to each other. They cannot be handed about any more than toothaches or headaches can. Each person must make his own thought for himself; no one else can make it for him. I open a book. Is there any thought there? Not a bit, there are only little black marks upon a white page. If I am unfamiliar with that particular system of marks I can make nothing out of them. I cannot even make them into sounds. I go to a lecture. Does any wisdom pass from speaker to listener there ? No; sound waves are vibrating the air. They fall upon my ear and I may be able to make something significant out of them, but if they are parts of a sound system which I do not know, I cannot. Again, the words may be familiar but the thought be strange. The speaker may be talking about the geometry of w-dimensional space, and, while I can make something out of every separate word, I can make no clear meaning out of his sentences or his discourse as a whole. I could, of course, learn to repeat his words after him, but I would still not know his meanings because I cannot make them in terms of my own experience.

1 Plato, Phasdrus (Jowett's translation), 274, 275.

No, language does not convey thought, and instruction cannot convey or supply knowledge. Plato was right. It is not something which can be thrust into the mind from outside like turnips into a turnip barrel. Conversation, lectures, and books may challenge us to think, provoke, invite to, or occasion thought, but they cannot supply it. Yes, you perhaps are saying, we admit that one must keep his eyes open and his ears attentive or he can appropriate nothing. While that is true," that is not what I mean.

Knowledge getting is not appropriating. I am trying to say that knowledge-getting can never be an appropriating any more than health or skill in boxing can be. One cannot learn to box unless he himself parries and gives the blows. One cannot have health except as health results from what he himself does. Just so, one cannot have knowledge unless he makes it for himself. You converse with me. I hear your words, but I must supply meanings for them out of my stock of experiences. I study Euclid's geometry. It is simply an occasion for me to make my own geometry. I must conceive a point, a line, a plane, a solid. I must be persuaded of the unprovable truth of the axioms and must postulate the postulates. I must appreciate the force of geometrical proof. I must feel the necessity of regarding the sum of the anglesof a triangle as two right angles. I must make all the truths of geometry out of my own conviction.

The process is the same in kind but not in degree in the case of every form of learning. It is sometimes said that Shakespeare shares his truth and Raphael and Bellini their religious and poetic insight with us, that the meaning of history and geography we do not make, but simply take. Can this be true ? If Shakespeare shares his meaning with us, why do some say that Hamlet was mad and others that he was not mad ? To Shakespeare he must either have been mad, or not mad, or both together, and if we simply take Shakespeare's meaning it must be only one of these three that we can hold, and Hamlet should mean the same definite personality to us that he did to Shakespeare. There would be no room for scholars' quarrels if truth were handed down to us in that way. But note that in the case even of Bible truth making so overshadows taking that the sects of Christianity are almost as numerous as those who ate of the loaves and the fishes. Again, if we do not make, but only share Shakespeare's perception of the truth of Hamlet, how does it happen that every actor who essays that great role gives us his own interpretation of it ? It must be that each makes his own conception of Hamlet out of the signs which Shakespeare set down to serve asmaterial for our construction. What Shakespeare's Hamlet was we shall never know, for the lines do not provide us enough clues to enable us to answer all our questions. The far greater service that he has rendered, the service every artist, inventor, lawgiver, and teacher renders, is just the one that my friend renders when he converses with me; namely, that of providing materials of experience for me to interpret, not with the hope that our meanings will coincide, but that starting upon somewhat the same quest and each using the appercep- tive material which past experience has enabled him to acquire, we shall each of us create a meaning which will be of value to us. The artist, according to Tolstoy, is one who can so use his material as to beget in the spectator the consciousness or awareness that he himself desired the spectator to experience. He comes to each one with a challenge, " See .in this, if you can, the meaning which I see in it." Thus the interpreter is a poet no less certainly than the poet whose words he interprets. Their difference is in degree of creative ability and not that one is a taker and the other a giver.

History is what we make of the past. When we come to history the same truth holds. What is the history of Greece? Is it a something that we merely find ready-made and which therefore wemust take and keep just as we found it, or is it a quarry to which each of us may go for many blocks of marble from which to shape the edifice of experience which he is building ? Grote went to it for one purpose, Shelley for another, and Keats for a third. Professor Person's purpose was very different from theirs. Each selected what he would, and each tells us what the Greeks were in terms of his interest. The absolute history of the Greeks can never be written. We shall have to be satisfied with the relativists' account, which is only another way of saying that the writing of history, like the studying of history, is a form of human creating. The student knows that to answer the question, Wherein were the Romans a different kind of people from the Greeks? he must first comprehend the import of the question and must then hunt for and select the passages in history which suggest the answer, and not only must he read his own meaning into the print which he finds in the library but he must assemble particular experiences of contrasting types of people. All of which leads him to shape some sort of more or less definite images, which he clothes, the one with one set of meanings and the other with the other, and calls the one the Greeks and the other the Romans.

In our study of geography it is particularly plain that each of us is engaged in building a worldimage. The notion that we must, for the sake of comprehension, begin with the familiar experiences of home geography verifies that statement of our process.

Education is world building. Education, then, we may regard as the process by which we make the " big blooming buzzing confusion " of feeling with which we started into an arranged world of things, each of which is a grouping of more or less definite feelings, a " permanent possibility of sensations."

This process has been going on for years when the child first comes to school. He has been experiencing at first hand both things and persons, and his feelings of them have already been pretty well schematized. Perceptual experience he has had in abundance, and from the first he has been grouping it into kinds or concepts. What must now be done ? A number of things. His first-hand perceiving must go on to the end of his days, and his classifying of his experiences into kinds must go on, too. But now he must learn to analyze his percepts and pick out those parts of them which will give him most control over his experience getting. The letters which he sees are black have a certain size as well as a certain shape and order; but he must learn to neglect their color and their size and fix his seeing upon their shape and theirgrouping in order to learn to read. The objects which he numbers, too, have size, weight, color, smoothness, or roughness. But he must learn to disregard these aspects of them in order to see them as ones and deal with them from the standpoint of numbers. He must learn to think about things in new and usable ways, and he must learn to think about thoughts. But in all this it is out of his own feeling that his world is to be built, and he only can do the building. We are prone to think that textbooks and teachers and schools, if they are but good enough, can do that work for him I that his learning can be conferred upon him from the outside. Forsooth, does not Shakespeare give us our poetry, Euclid our geometry, Darwin our biology, and somewhat less distinguished men our other forms of knowledge ? The notion is a popular one, and the view opposed to it has clothed itself in such thought-obscuring phrases as that education is a process of self-activity or of self-realization, with the result that the crude mistaken notion almost holds the field.

The function of the school. But if each one of us must do his own world building for himself, must see with his own eyes, hear with his own ears, image with his own imagination, classify according to his own purposes, and be convinced of logical necessity through his own feeling ofconviction, can the school do anything that is really worth while for him ? If he must do all his learning for himself, why send him to school at all ? The answer, and so far as I can see, the only answer which can be given to this question, is that the school can do only one thing I it can offer a carefully selected environment in reaction to which the learner will use his own mind in socially profitable ways. The teacher is the chief factor in this social environment.

He represents society's insistence upon order, work, and accomplishment. He is by no means there as a purveyor of knowledge but as a fellow worker in the search for socially profitable ways to use the mind. It is repeated over and over again that the teacher must be a model to the child, and by this is usually meant that the teacher's moral conduct must be a model; but what the phrase really means is that the teacher must furnish an example of interest in knowledge-making and in the use of mind in solving the problems of human life. If he would have his students use their minds in the developing of their bodies, in the shaping of their conduct or in the making of other forms of knowledge, he must lead the way. Again, the subjects of study upon which teacher and pupils are engaged are only a series of challenges to think out the social experience which they formulate and to find out, each by the useA his own apperceiving experience, if what they declare is not so. They present social experience through the medium of textbooks, each of which i nothing but a book of texts, presented in sym-]n for which the students are to make meanings and about which they are to weave their own texture of experience, both sensory and motor, in much the same way as does the preacher in his efforts to expound his theme.

The use of workshops, laboratories, problems, the preparation of papers, the taking of examinations, together with devices for student self-government, etc. I all are but efforts to provide an environment in which the student shall work out his own experience into more usable capitalized forms.

According to this conception "education is'not for life, but it is life." It cannot be a preparation for life without being life. A specially selected environment the school must be, but an environment selected from life itself and not made out of another kind of needs, problems, surroundings, and demands than life itself presents. Artificial to a degree it must be, but artificial in the same sense that the family and the state are artificial; that is, that they are human arrangements for doing the real work of the world and not devices for superfluous tasks which could just as well be done without.

From this standpoint the school is the "green meadow " wherein there are " samples of lives," and the teachers are the guardians of the " samples of lives." The generations, as they are born, advance to the meadow and, with the assistance of the teachers, each one selects the life which appeals to him most and goes upward " to live it a hundred years." But it is his own life that he selects, his own world of meanings that he here is allowed special opportunities to reflectively interpret. *De te fabula narratur* is the form in which every discourse must be addressed to him. And what is sought must ever be his own interpretation, his own insight, his own making of values.

Education, then, is the process by which the individual continues the preschool activity of getting experience and working it over by reflection into terms of social utility. It is a process which he does not begin in the school and cannot end when he leaves the school. It is essentially the life process and the work of life., Plato was right, therefore, when he spoke of education as a life work. Experience must continue to function in the getting of new experience, and old experience must continually be reinterpreted to meet new experience. The process of learning must be kept up; without that, even the capitalized experience of facts and methods of handling them, which we have thus far succeeded in accumulating, willslip away, for one cannot acquire any form of skill and discontinue it without in large measure losing it. It is not surprising, therefore, that some young people forget how to read four or five years after leaving school, that others forget how to add, and still others how to write or to spell. There is no known way of teaching any form of action so that the person who has once learned it will continue, without further effort, to be able to perform it as long as he lives. There is only one form of insurance against the lapsing of one's acquirements, no matter what they are. They cannot be wrapped in the napkin of forgetfulness and carefully laid away. They must be put to use. The schools which regard education as a result and not as a process raise false hopes in the minds of their students. In reality they have to do only with the apprentice stages of each of the forms of activity with which they are concerned. They have a duty to make it particularly clear to all who come under their instruction that they cannot enable one to acquire permanent habits, or a knowledge which will not run away, if special efforts are not made to continue the process of interpreting experience which the student has only begun.

On the other hand, one cannot be a master workman in any field without engaging himself in a constant effort to enlarge his knowledge ofthat field. My professor of ethics used to say that "the good man who merely repeats his goodness of the day before is not a good man, but a bad man." The good teacher or the good physician or the good carpenter who merely repeat their goodness of the day before are not good but bad workmen. Why? Because every day is a new day with its new demands upon us, and we must grow in grace and likewise in knowledge in order to meet them. There is no form of knowledge so complete and final that it cannot be improved, no single human art so perfect that it cannot be made better, no form of human endeavor that does not call for further effort. For this philosophy, life is a perfecting, not an arriving at perfections, and the joy is in the process, not in reaching and remaining at a goal.

5

SECTION 5

CHAPTER V
THE KINDS OF EDUCATION

The only kind of education. If our analysis is correct the only kind of education that there is is self-education. It is not a thing of fixed subjects of instruction. No one study and no particular group of studies is indispensable. Neither is attendance at any particular kind of school, though the likelihood is a bit greater that if one has surrounded himself with inducements to study he will be a little more certain to study because of them than in their absence. It is a true saying, however, and worthy of general credence, that "many are exposed to an education but few take it." / Education is the process by which each individual / out of his own awareness builds his world. No one can see, hear, taste, touch, smell, walk, or talk for the child. He must do all these things for himself. Just so, no one can image for him, remember for him, think for him, will for him. But human beings have been so busily engaged in doing these things before he came, and have so successfully recorded the experiences which they have had in doing them, that he seems to be surrounded by a world of ready-made existences and meanings which require no building up through constructive experience on his part, but only appropriation. Just what images are in the minds of those who advance the notion that education is appropriation it is hard to make out. Yet educators do sometimes talk as though they believed the child was freed from the necessity of learning to walk because the race has walked, or the necessity of seeing, handling, and experimenting with what the race has, out of such experience, learned to call objects because it has given them names, or by trial and error to find out how to conduct himself because the race has already learned by experimenting how to conduct itself. This conception of education views it as a body of results to be imparted without going through the processes which lead to them. Whenever education is conceived in that fashion, an impossible task is undertaken, and an outcome of no profit but of positive harm, both to the learner and to society which attempts to teach him thus, is inevitable.

The nature of our social inheritance. Must each learner then begin at the very beginning just as the race did and rediscover all that it has discovered for himself? Is it of no advantage to him to be born late in the course of civilization ? Shall he not profit by what has already been found out?Certainly he will profit and profit greatly, yet not by appropriating results merely but by appropriating results through their processes.

Our social inheritance is an inheritance of methods. The wise invite us not to see with their eyes or to think with their minds, but to look with our own eyes and to think with our own minds upon those matters of great concern to men with which they busied themselves and in their experimenting found profitable ways of treating them, standpoints of advantage, and methods which may lead to control. Professor Baldwin has made a distinction of first-rate importance in designating the world which we are born into as our social inheritance. To be born into a German family does not mean that one brings with him a structural tendency to learn the German language, but it does mean that he inherits an environment in which he must learn to communicate in German. His situation provides a particular form of activity for his mind to work in. German does not come to him without his laying hold of it word by word and sentence by sentence. He is the inheritor of a way of speaking. He cannot well escape communicating with those about him in the words which they use, but to do so he must reinvent the language because of their occasioning him to do so. He inherits the race's knowledge in the same way. It is to him but a languagewhich he must learn to use if he would communicate with his fellow men and have their help in living. It comes to him not as a fixed body of ready-made truth which he can take without creating. It is only an occasion, an opportunity, and, to an extent, a necessity for his own mental activity. His mother spoke in German, and showed him the way and put him under the necessity of developing a system of meanings for her sound symbols and of himself using a similar system of sounds. Instruction in language, literature, science, history, or philosophy can do nothing more; they are simply invitations to him to perfect his own awareness, suggestions as to problems that the race has met in its course and which he will most likely meet in his, and intimations of ways in which he will find it profitable to attack them. He may learn this language of the sciences just as he may learn German with degrees of mastery. He may be able to repeat its words without feeling their meanings. He may be able to read it without being able to write it, or to understand it without uttering it. He may collect a great store of curious and interesting facts about it and not be able to use it, or he may be able to think in it and to speak it. But the prime fact about the language is that it was made to think by and to speak with, and this is the prime fact about all forms of human learning.They are tools. They were made for use. That is their reason for being. No matter how much custom and convention may overload them with other meanings, use is their sole reality.

What the task of the educator is. The task of the educator is a strange one. He must so act upon others that they will feel, think, and act for themselves. What he himself does, no matter how perfectly, is never the end which he seeks. The instruments with which he works I the knowledge which the race has already attained I are not the end either. Like himself and his acts they are but means also. The feeling, the conviction, the reaction of the man inside the learner, is the one thing needful, is the aim of all our striving.

Are studies elementary and higher? We are prone to think of studies as having other objects than these. Convention has divided them into higher and lower forms, and taught the world to regard some kinds of knowledge as noble with a nobility not their own and others as base with a baseness which does not belong to them. The same unthinking convention has led teachers and students alike to treat certain studies as concerns only of the early years of life, and other studies as belonging only to the later years. Teachers are apt to take pride in the fact that they teach " the higher studies " and the lack of it in the fact thatthey teach the "lower" ones. If our pride is a product of our service, should it not be just the other way round ? The so-called elementary studies are elementary to human activity, not to our school years. All the great arts represent the chief interests of the race and must be begun in early years and continued through life. The teacher of reading and writing thinks perhaps that hers is a menial task. But " with the art of writing," says Carlyle, "the true reign of miracles for mankind commenced. If we think of it, all that a university can do for us is still what the first school began doing I teach us to read." And every university teacher is constantly engaged in finding out whether or no his students can make for themselves the meaning which they are challenged to make by the printed page. Surely that is a process which cannot end on their part when they leave the university, but one which they must continue as long as they live. The problem of instruction in reading is not to teach people how to read but to read I a very different undertaking and one which lasts a lifetime. Writing too is much more than the shaping of letters. That is only its beginning. " Writing maketh an exact man," said Bacon. We misconceive its character when we take it in its lowest terms. No wonder the business man finds fault with handwriting unrelated to compositionand unspecialized by purpose. Our students have learned to copy copies or to write a write, but rarely to write a letter or a bill of sale or a set of accounts. If the psychologists are correct in saying that adolescence disorganizes even this aspect of the handwriting of children, it would seem that the study of penmanship also cannot successfully be completed in the elementary school. When we begin mathematics we must deal with the most abstract of all the aspects of reality. We must look away from the stuff of the objects which we count in order to count them. We are ever more concerned with quality than with quantity. For this reason William T. Harris regarded arithmetic as a relatively unfruitful study. " What is the habit of thought worth which is trained to neglect the quality, that is, the essential nature of objects?" I he asks. Plainly habituation in quantitative reckoning will not of itself make us expert discriminators of qualities. To distinguish food from poison, silk from cotton, truth from falsity, right from wrong, we must have learned by experience the many degrees and the marks of each of these things. Mathematics does not profess to deal with real things in their concreteness, but it does guide us to real things by considering aspects which they always present in such uniform

1 Annual Report of the Board of Education, p. 29, St. Louis, 1910.

ways as to open up pathways of experience. It is a language which tells us of experiences which we may have in the future in terms of the experiences which we have already had. Because it makes a very small part stand for the whole, that is, prefigures experiences by very dim aspects which are correspondingly easy to isolate, its application is the most far-reaching of all the phases of scientific method.

We cannot regard our first lessons in the use of this difficult language of abstractions as easy. The mere mnemonic jugglery of symbols may not be difficult, but that is only the superficial part of the operation. These concepts have been formulated to enable us to dip up experiences. To know arithmetic does not mean merely to know how to use it, but to know to use it, just as to have learned reading means not to know how to read but to read. Such a laying. hold of one of the chief tools which mind has shaped for its work cannot be accomplished in the few short years of the elementary-school course. It requires a lifetime of effort. Facility in even the simplest operations slips away unless what is acquired in the primary school is continued in the college. If we would remember poetry, we must not only commit it, but we must continue to repeat it. The musician and the athlete must train for each performance.The marksman may be able to hit the bull's-eye this year, but unless he keeps in practice he will be but an indifferent shot some months hence. Like these, facility in numbering is an art that cannot be acquired once for all so as to last a lifetime. Spelling, too, is an accomplishment that requires the persistent use of the dictionary. History and geography are life interests. Our knowledge of them should expand in after-school years, but even the elements run away from us unless we keep renewing them. Language we are ever learning. The lower school begins the analysis of these great racial activities; the higher schools but continue what it has begun.

Are studies properly classified as instrumental and cultural? Studies are sometimes divided into instrumental and cultural. It is difficult to comprehend the reason for such a classification. The theory which is behind it is that some studies contain and supply knowledge while others are but tools which we must use in getting it. But knowledge, as we have seen, cannot reside in books or be transmitted by one person to another. Books, schools, teachers, even sciences themselves, are only its raw materials, opportunities for the activity of the learner to develop a living awareness. From this standpoint every study is only a path for him to walk in, a road so marked out and signboardedby the experience of his fellow men that he need not make the wasteful preliminary explorations and chartings which they were compelled to make but in which he must do his own walking for himself, for neither they nor anyone else can carry him upon their shoulders. Every study, then, is a series of standpoints to be taken, of problems to be solved, of experiences to be relived. Why? Because the experience which is to come is going to be like the experience which the learner has in pursuing it. He must use the experience which he already has in interpreting it, and the life which he lives and the experience which he gets in pursuing it, in the interpretation of new experience and the consequent reinterpretation of old experience as long as he is alive. He learns to read, but no matter how much we may congratulate ourselves upon his literacy, unless his knowledge is of such a sort that it puts itself into practice neither he nor we will be the better for it. It is a favorite saying of the philosophers nowadays that reality is that which makes a difference to the systematic procedure of human nature. Education must be measured by the same foot rule. Unless it makes a difference, a very real difference, in the systematic procedure of human nature, it is not education. True education intends to make men producers of a certain kind of life.

Is history an instrumental study ? Reading, writing, and arithmetic are regarded as instrumental studies. They present a series of acts to be performed. But history, it is said, is not a tool. It is ja cultural study. Through it we are led to contemplate the growth of the concept of liberty, the forming of the nation, the battles for its preservation, the development of its industries, the wholesome ordering of its life. We must look upon these things because the spectacle will be pleasing to us and will do us good. But if this were all or nearly all which came from this or any other study, it would be a profaning of opportunity to rob youth of its years for so trifling a purpose. What is real makes a difference, but this is taken as though it made no difference. If we are taught the traditions of the nation, I not forsooth because there happen to be traditions and we happen to be learners and because convention has said to our otherwise unoccupied teachers that this is as good a way as any to fill an idle hour, but for the reason that Niceratus' father caused him to get every line of Homer by heart, that is, to make a moral man of him, I it would seem that history is an instrumental and not a cultural study. If it teaches us the use of tools, our country, her necessities, our citizenship, what the master workmen who made her thought of her, hoped for her, and did for her, then surely this

knowledge is as practical as that of copying letters or pronouncing words. Our country is not an outside entity which exists apart from the consciousness of its people. It is and always has been a life, a human arrangement, unescapable to be sure, but having the particular form which it has because of the intentions of men. It is essentially a social tool, a partnership which everyone must enter, and, to do so, must be taught the objects of the partnership ; and what has been accomplished by it to date. I sometimes ask my students to answer the question, Where is the United States ? Is it the land bounded by the Atlantic on the east, the Pacific on the west, Canada on the north, and Mexico on the south? No, that is the territory of the United States. That was all here before Columbus came, and not one inch of it can pass away, though the United States may pass away. Perhaps then the United States is at Washington where the President, the Supreme Court, and the Congress are? No, that is the government of the United States. The United States is in the hearts of its people. It is a thought, a hope, a resolution. It is always .becoming, it never is. It is recreated anew when each one of its people catches the vision. That is the reason why the foreigner from another birthplace may become as real a citizen as the native born. It is a unity of minds to realize a common

purpose, a great cooperative undertaking. Can what it has been when reflected upon be other than a means for what it shall be? History is our initiation into the guild of citizens. Every part of the liturgy has meaning and cries to us to hearken to its significance. It must deal with facts and nothing but facts, but its facts are meanings.

What is science? Science also is a human institution. It is only a specially persistent attempt to use past and present experience to anticipate coming experience, due to the conviction that the experience of the future will be like that of the past. We reduce our experience up to date to formulas, concepts, laws, dropping out its time-and-placeness and omitting all such particularity from it in these general statements. We face forward. " Belief in a general statement," says W. K. Clifford,1 " is an artifice of our mental constitution, whereby infinitely various sensations and groups of sensations are brought into connection with infinitely various actions and groups of actions. . . . The important point is that science, though apparently transformed into pure knowledge, has yet never lost its character of being a *craft;* and that it is not the knowl-. edge itself which can rightly be called science, but a special way of getting and using knowledge. Namely, science is the getting of knowledge from

1 Clifford, Lectures and Essays, Vol. II, p. 77. London, 1901.

experience on the assumption of uniformity in nature, and the use of such knowledge to guide the actions of men. And the most abstract statements or propositions in science are to be regarded as bundles of hypothetical maxims packed into portable shape and size. Every scientific fact is a shorthand expression for a vast number of practical directions: if you want so and so, do so and so."

Of like tenor is the statement of Professor W. S. Franklin, quoted by Professor James: " I think that the sickliest notion of physics, even if a student gets it, is that it is ' the science of masses, molecules, and the ether,' and I think that the healthiest notion, even if a student does not wholly get it, is that physics is the science of the ways of taking hold of bodies and pushing them."1

Is literature an instrumental study ? When we come to the classics, pragmatic education meets a stiff bulwark. Shall immemorial dignity be forced to give the countersign of the market place ? Shall that which is ancient and established take its place along with the provisional, the temporary, the instrumental ? Surely here, if anywhere, is art for art's sake, knowledge for knowledge's sake. " That ideal ' professor of education,'" Matthew Arnold, made a careful analysis of their value, which isall too much neglected. " Meanwhile neither our humanists nor our realists adequately conceive the circle of knowledge, and each party is unjust to all that to which its own aptitudes do not carry it. The humanists are loath to believe that man has any access to vital knowledge except by knowing himself, I the poetry, philosophy, history which his spirit has created; the realists, that he has any access except by knowing the world, I the physical sciences, the phenomena and laws of nature. I, like so many others who have been brought up in the old routine, imperfectly as I know letters,Ithe work of the human spirit itself, I know nothing else, and my judgment therefore may fairly be impeached. But it seems to me that so long as the realists persist in cutting in two the circle of knowledge, so long do they leave for practical purposes the better portion to their rivals, and in the government of human affairs their rivals will beat them. And for this reason. The study of letters is the study of the operation of human force, of human freedom and activity; the study of nature is the study of the operation of non-human forces, of human limitation and passivity.

The contemplation of human force and activity tends naturally to heighten our own force and activity; the contemplation of human limits and passivity tends rather to check it. Therefore the men who have had thehumanistic training have played, and yet play, so prominent a part in human affairs, in spite of their prodigious ignorance of the universe; because their training has powerfully fomented the human force in them. And in this way letters are indeed *runes,* like those magic runes taught by the Valkyrie Brynhild to Sigurd, the Scandinavian Achilles, which put the crown to his endowment and made him invincible.

1 *Science,* January 2, 1903.

" Still, the humanists themselves surfer so much from the ignorance of physical facts and laws, and from the inadequate conception of nature, and of man as a part of nature, I the conduct of human affairs suffers so much from the same cause, I that the intellectual insufficiency of the humanities, conceived as the one access to vital knowledge, is perhaps at the present moment yet more striking than their power of practical stimulation; and we may willingly declare with the Italians that no part of the circle of knowledge is common or unclean, none is to be cried up at the expense of another.... All the historical part of this volume has shown that the great movements of the human spirit have either not got hold of the public schools, or not kept hold of them. What reforms have been made have been patchwork, the work of able men who, into certain departments of school study which were dear to them, infused reality and life, but wholooked little beyond these departments and did not concern themselves with fully adjusting instruction to the wants of the human mind. There is, therefore, no intelligent tradition to be set aside in our public schools; there is only a routine, arising in the way we have seen, and destined to be superseded as soon as ever that more adequate idea of instruction, of which the modern spirit is even now in travail, shall be born.

" That idea, so far as one can already forecast its lineaments, will subordinate the matter and methods of instruction to the end in view; I the end of conducting the pupil, as I have said, through the means of his special aptitudes to a knowledge of himself and the world. The natural sciences are a necessary instrument of this knowledge; letters and *Alterthumswissenschaft* are a necessary instrument of this knowledge. But if school instruction in the natural sciences has almost to be created, school instruction in letters and *Alterthumswissenschaft* has almost to be created anew. The prolonged philological discipline, which in our present schools guards the access to *Alterthumswissenschaft,* brings to mind the philosophy of Albertus Magnus, the mere introduction to which I the logic, I was by itself enough to absorb all the student's time of study. . . . But many people have even convinced themselves that the preliminaryphilological discipline is so extremely valuable as to be an end in itself; and, similarly, that the mathematical discipline preliminary to a knowledge of nature is so extremely valuable as to be an end in itself. It seems to me that those who profess this conviction do not enough consider the quantity of knowledge inviting the human mind and the importance to the human mind of really getting to it. No preliminary discipline is to be pressed at the risk of keeping minds from getting at the main matter, a knowledge of themselves and the world... . No doubt it is indispensable to have exact habits of mind, and mathematics and grammar are excellent for the promotion of these habits; and Latin, besides having so large a share in so many modern languages, offers a grammar which is the best of all grammars for this promotion. Here are valid reasons for making every schoolboy learn some Latin and some mathematics, but not for turning the preliminary matter into the principal, and sacrificing every aptitude except that for the science of language or of pure mathematics. A Latin grammar of thirty pages and the most elementary treatise of arithmetic and of geometry, would amply suffice for the uses of philology and mathematics as a universally imposed preparatory discipline. By keeping within these strict limits, absolute exactness of knowledge, | the habit which is hereour professed aim, | might be far better attained than it is at present. But it is well to insist, besides, that all knowledge may and should, when we have got fit teachers for it, be so taught as to promote exact habits of mind; and we are not to take leave of these when we pass beyond our introductory discipline. But it is sometimes said that only through close philological studies and the close practice of Latin and Greek composition can *Alterthumswissenchaft* itself, the science of the ancient world, be truly reached. It is said to be only through these that we get really to know Greek and Latin literature. For all practical purposes this proposition is untrue, and its untruth can be easily tested.... I cannot help thinking, therefore, that the modern spirit will deprive Latin and Greek composition and verbal scholarship of their present universal and preponderant application in our secondary schools, and will make them as practiced in their present high scale, *Privatstudien,* as the Germans say, for boys with an eminent aptitude for them."1

Is this education for efficiency? The object of education of all sorts, then, would seem to be to enable the student to get such a grip upon himself and the world of men and of things that he can usewhat he has learned in making his life function. Is this education for efficiency? That altogether depends on how you define *efficiency.* It is one thing to strive to equip a mind to function well in its present environment and as long as that environment remains static, and quite another to equip it to make over its environment and to make over its own responses to meet a rapidly changing social life. The doctrine of evolution has taught us to say that education is adjustment to environment, but it is still too often overlooked that environment itself grows, is dynamic, and ever running away from us. Education must not only fit the individual to it but to keep up with it. It must not only enable him to adjust himself as nearly perfectly as may be but to readjust himself and keep readjusting himself as long as he lives. Besides, he must do his part in remaking it to fit his own and the needs of his fellows. Like the Athenian ephebe he must be solemnly dedicated to the task of leaving his country and the world greater and better than they were when committed to him. Each one must be trained to pull his own weight and not to prevent his fellow from pulling his; that is, each one must be able to buy his living from society and must not interfere with his neighbor as he buys his, and in addition, each one must by his effort raise the standard of living bothfor himself and for his group. That he may have inherited wealth or position does not exempt him. His active nature and his membership in the group both require him to work his way by performing his share of service.

1 Arnold, Higher Schools and Universities in Germany, chap. viii, pp. 172-181. London, 1874.

Liberal versus *illiberal education.* There is one ancient distinction which a slave-holding civilization introduced into education, which society based upon a caste system has retained, but which a people that takes democracy seriously is sure to banish. It is the distinction which Aristotle bequeathed to the ages when he wrote, " There can be no doubt that children should be taught those useful things which are really necessary, but not all things; for occupations are divided into liberal and illiberal; and to young children should be imparted only such kinds of knowledge as will be useful to them without vulgarizing them. And any occupation, art, or science which makes the body or soul or mind of the freeman less fit for the practice or exercise of virtue, is vulgar; wherefore, we call those arts vulgar which tend to deform the body, and likewise all paid employments, for they absorb and degrade the mind. There are also some liberal arts quite proper for a freeman to acquire, but only in a certain degree, and if he attend to them too closely, in order to attain perfection in them, the same evil effects will follow. The object also which a mansets before him makes a great difference: if he does or learns anything for his own sake, or for the sake of his friends, or with a view to excellence, the action will not appear illiberal; but if done for the sake of others, the very same action will be thought menial and servile."1 The necessity of preserving status by learning nothing in the way that a slave would learn it sticks out in every sentence of this distinction.

Stoic reflection attempted to give the notion of liberal education another meaning. It strove to revise the import of the phrase "liberal studies." To the objection that a slave should not pursue philosophy Seneca replies, "Is he a slave? but perchance a freeman in mind. Is he a slave ? Show me one who is not."2 " Studies are called liberal because they are worthy of a free man. But there is one study which is liberal indeed, which maketh a man free, and that is wisdom, high, valiant and magnanimous; the others are petty and childish things. . . . The mind is made perfect by one thing only, by the unchanging knowledge of good and evil which philosophy imparts."3 The phrase " a liberal education " still keeps a trace of the connotation which Aristotle gave it. It means not merely a liberalizing education, but also thatkind of education which most becomes the proud children of those who claim to be the nobler class. It is a question begging designation. If we describe one kind of education as liberal, we do not dare to say that another kind is illiberal, for no education can be that. We do not say it, but our phrase implies it. Even if the phrase did not have this backhanded tendency, its denotation is so indefinite as to make it worthless. All real education is liberal, for all real education makes men free, and all real education is for service. The phrase "a liberal education " has an historic significance, but no present-day applicability. It is too outworn and defective a bottle to hold the new wine of democratic endeavor.

1 Aristotle, Politics (Jowett's translation), 1337 f.

2 Seneca, Epistle 47. Ibid. Epistle 88.

Is education properly classified as vocational and avocational? Since education is for service, it is throughout vocational. Half the ills of mankind come from the misuse of words, according to Socrates. In recent years an effort has been made to give this good old word *vocation* a narrow technical meaning, which neither its history, its etymology, nor the needs of the science of education will bear. " Vocational education," we are told, " is any education the controlling purpose of which is to fit for a gainful occupation." Etymo- logically, one's vocation is one's calling. When the author of the Epistle to the Hebrews salutedthose to whom he wrote as " partakers of the heavenly calling," and St. Paul urged the men of Corinth each to " abide in the same calling wherein he was called," they were speaking to them about their vocations. When Fichte wrote on " The Vocation of Man " and Emerson gave his famous address on the " Vocation of the Scholar," they were not using that word in the sense of " a gainful occupation." One's profession is not a vocation until it invites his whole energy and takes possession of his spirit. That is the meaning which the word has in literature. It signifies the purpose to which one devotes his life. There can be no question that the gaining of a livelihood is an essential part of the vocation of everyone. But there are other parts just as essential, or perhaps even more essential, in the vocation of the human being. Those who seek to restrict the meaning of this word to trade training, industrial teaching, or special instruction, which prepares for a gainful occupation, divide education into two kinds with it I vocational education and avocational education. Vocational education is that education which prepares for a gainful occupation. All the rest is avocational, they say I which is a short and easy way of using words to discredit the importance of all other forms of instruction. Human activity cannot be exhaustively classified as vocational andavocational without making one's avocation more important than one's vocation. One's avocation calls him away from his regular duties. It is that secondary purpose which is pursued from sheer interest without the constraint of necessity. Is citizenship vocational or avocational? Is being a good neighbor, a good member of a family? In one sense one is called to these things more imperatively than he is called to make a living, for the state removes him from society if he fails to prepare himself to meet its requirements in these directions, while it provides him a living and lets him go free, if he is unable to make it for himself. Again " no man would choose the possession of all goods in the world on the condition of solitariness, man being a social animal and formed by nature for living with others."1 Preparation for these life interests is essentially vocational, for they are constituent parts of the vocation of man. It is a preparation for necessary human working, but not for money-gaining working merely.

Recognition of the fact that vocational education must be wider than trade training is furnished by the action of the school authorities of Edinburgh, Scotland, who combine four elements in their scheme of vocational training: (i) training for occupation, (2) training in the English language,(3) training in citizenship, (4) physical training. " Education for a calling," says Dr. Kerschensteiner, "offers us the very best foundation for the general education of a man. We are far too much inclined to assume both in the old world and in the new, that it is possible to educate a man without reference to some special calling. . . . Yet it lies in our power to make an education for a calling as many sided as any education can be. ... Industry is not the aim of human society. The aim of society is the increase of justice and culture. . . . The schools are not merely technical or trade schools. They only make use of the pupil's trade as the basis of their educational work. The trade training which they give is not the object of the school. However thorough this training in a continuation school, for instance, in Munich, is, it is only the starting point for the wider general training for the education in practical and theoretical thinking, in consideration for others, in devotion to common interests, in social service for the state and community." 1 A definite terminology is highly important for education, but arbitrary usage must not be allowed to transform words which have had a vital significance through the ages into narrowlytechnical terms. There are other terms which have been used to designate gainful labor, such as trades, industries, occupations, etc. The education which prepares specifically for them is properly designated as trade, industrial, or occupational training. Of itself it does not constitute vocational education, though it forms a necessary part of it. That term should be. saved to designate the purposive training for human living which all real education seeks to develop. Our contention, however, is not for the word but for the meaning. Genuine education of all sorts is either specifically preparatory or must become so. Trade instruction has no monopoly of this quality and must not be allowed to seem to have.

1 Aristotle, Ethics, Bk. IX, Sect JMi

[166] -

1 Three Lectures on Vocational Training by Dr. Georg Kerschensteiner, published by the Commercial Club of Chicago, 1911. Lecture I, pp. 2-9.

One must be trained to make a living; that does not mean that he can live by bread alone, and assuredly it does not mean that he can live without fit. Much of the so-called industrial education has 1 no other purpose than the making of boys and girls into hands. Much of the so-called cultural education makes dependents. Real education is satisfied with neither of these results. It strives to make self-sustaining persons. We may name its parts by distinctive names such as cultural instruction and technical or trade training, but they are all parts of one indispensable whole of preparation, not alternative species of education.

According to this analysis, we should recognize but one kind and various degrees of education, the broad and the narrow, or, when looked at from the standpoint of time, the long course and the short one. The object is the same for everyone, that is, the conscious reorganizing of experience in order to shape it into the best possible tool with which to anticipate and meet the future. There is none too much wisdom in our forefathers' outlook, none too much first-hand experience which we ourselves can have with men and things, none too much stocking of our minds with the insight and the plans which the race has worked out in its efforts to meet the needs of life and which we may make our own by reliving them. Conditions of aptitude and opportunity force some of us to be satisfied with the narrower course, and others to demand the wider training, but the difference is in degree, not in kind.

6

SECTION 6

CHAPTER VI
LEARNING BY AND FOR DOING

Learning for doing. The student lives in three tenses. Behind him and about him is the world which his fellow men have learned to harness more or less successfully to their needs. About him and in front of him is the world which he must harness more successfully than they did. For he must not merely repeat their achievements of the days before; in him the race must grow in grace to meet the ever new demands of a living universe. For our purposes we may image life as one vast shop with the raw stuff which is to be worked into more serviceable shapes lying all about and the tools with which it is to be worked hanging in profusion from the walls. The master workman is busy at his task, and his apprentices beside him are learning their trade by helping him. They must acquire it not merely by rule of thumb, though, for the ways of working iron which are employed are imperfect and better ways must be found out; besides there are better metals than iron for many of the purposes for which we use it. One must master thecraft in such a way as to find out what they are and devise and adopt the requisite methods of working them.

Thus education throughout is a doing on the part of the learner. But what he learns to do as an apprentice is different from what he will do later as a master workman | different, but yet recognizably and functionally the same, for while both the sensory content and the motor response of his action will change, the new action will be only a readaptation of the old content and response which he learned to make when a similar sensory content presented itself. It is a taking of the most useful tools in the race's workshop by the student into his own hands and by his own trial and effort learning to use them, but in such a way that he will go on perfecting his skill in their use as long as he lives. Education, that is, seeks the impossible. It is forever engaged in helping each student to become a perpetual-motion machine, to start a process in such a way that it will continue itself to the end of the student's days.

Some forms of teaching in which the students doing is clearly the end sought. Fortunate are those teachers whose task is plain, who do not have to fight their way through a well-nigh impenetrable thicket of contradictory conceptions as to just what they are employed to do before they can set aboutdoing it . For what can be more despairing than to labor at an undefined task with the conviction heavy upon one that in spite of the fact that he does not know what must be done, the work upon which he is engaged is nevertheless the most serious thing in the world? Is it any wonder that the teacher's task is a consuming one! If he fails to understand it and falls back upon conventional notions of his duty, he does not educate; and if he strives to educate, he does not produce a conventional product. In either case he is ground between the millstones of dissatisfaction.

Happy indeed are those teachers of physical training whose task is simply to teach their students to do the things which bring health and bodily efficiency. When they give instruction in breathing, it is plain that the one object which they have is not to give their students a knowledge about breathing, but to get each one of them to use his own lungs in a health-giving fashion. When they teach them to sit and to stand and to walk, it is not merely a knowledge of how to do these things, but an actual doing of them that they must aim at. And when they teach them the setting-up exercises or to dance, to run, to swim, to wrestle, to box, to fence, to work on the bars, the rings, the horse, or with the weights, it is a doing on the part of the student that they seek | not a knowingmerely, but a doing accompanied, if possible, by such a comprehension of purpose, by such an interest in the process and such an awareness of increasing skill that the work will not be given up until habits of functioning shall have established themselves which may be relied upon to contribute their share to the physical well-being of the individual as long as he exists. It is difficult to think of a knowledge of physical training which could have any other function than to direct physical doing.

The aim of the teacher of the fine arts is almost equally clear. If he gives instruction in painting, singing, or the playing of an instrument, it is plain that the instructor must guide, but the student must perform; that no matter how much the master may know about the theory of the art, that knowledge will have meaning for the student and can be imparted to him only in connection with his own doing; that all formal lessons such as learning to read the score, finger exercises, the manipulation of the stops, the tuning of the instrument, etc. are but the necessary parts of a larger process and without significance by themselves. The skill which is sought is a habit, and not a habit in general, but a particular doing conditioned by its own particular body of sensory elements. This habit will not come as a by-product of general aimless familiarity with an instrument, but only by day-by-day striving to master its use. That mastery is never so complete that after any definite number of years of preparation the great pianist is at last able to play anything without any preliminary practice whatever, but even in the period of his greatest virtuosity he must still practice a number of hours each day to keep in form.

What is a general knowledge of music or athletics? Education has much to learn from those who train themselves consciously to marked degrees of skill. They are not confused by obscurity of purpose, there is little delusion among them as to what the teacher must do and what the pupil, they do not make the error of assuming that the best way to learn to play upon the piano is to begin with the violin, the relation of theory to practice is fairly plain to them, and there is but little mistaking of the procedure of habit forming or of the place and function of interest in learning. They do not split the sensory-motor arc by saying that the purpose of instruction is to acquire methods of working with one subject matter in order to apply them to another. With them every subject matter calls for its own series of reactions, and every series of motor activities is called forth by its own unique perceptual series. To be sure, there are general terms, common elements in athletics as well as in music, but what kind of a knowledge of music does anyone possess who has only a general and no particular knowledge of it? And what kind of an athlete is he who has a general knowledge of athletics but no particular form of athletic skill ? The general grows out of the particular and cannot exist apart from it. A general training is either a combination of several particular forms of training such as would enable a musician to play upon several different instruments, or an athlete to contest in several different kinds of athletic events, or it is such a nondescript and puerile knowledge about these fields as to be synonymous merely with a vague acquaintance with them. A general education is sometimes spoken of as an all-round training. An all-round athlete is one who is proficient in several forms of athletic skill, and an all-round musician is one who is proficient in several kinds of musical skill. But in what forms of skill is the man who has pursued an all-round education proficient ?

Knowing comes from doing. It will not do to say that he knows many things but cannot do them. Awareness and doing cannot be separated thus. The sensory-motor arc is one. Neither function can exist without the other. Wherever there is sensory experience there is motor action, and wherever there is doing it brings its quota of awareness. If the knowledge is poor and mean, that is because the doing has been poor and mean which preconditioned it. To know anything without being able to do it is to know it poorly. One does not have to be a sugar planter to know that sugar tastes sweet, but he does have to taste it. One does not have to play in the orchestra to know that its music is voicing the unutterable, but he does have to listen to it, not once but many times until he begins to comprehend its language. There is a difference between appreciation and production, but it does not lie in the fact that appreciation is a passive state while production is a doing. Both are active states; their difference is in degree of comprehension rather than in kind. All knowledge is preconditioned by a doing on the part of the learner. The text of the New Testament | " If any man will do his will, he shall know of the doctrine " | might well be used as a motto to indicate what is required in all forms of education.

One's knowledge grows in proportion to one's doing. The sugar planter knows sugar more thoroughly than the merchant who sells it or the person who consumes it, for he also sells and consumes it. The person who merely reads about it does something that gives him an experience of it, but his relation to it is so remote that unless his awareness can take on an intenser form it can hardly be called knowledge. It is " experience " which " makesthe days of men to proceed according to art and inexperience according to chance, and different' persons in different ways are proficient in different arts."

It is the accumulated purposive doings of the race which have defined the problems, shaped the hypotheses, collected the evidence to prove and disprove them, and formulated the provisional conclusions which we call science. Its doctrines, no matter how seemingly conclusive, still wait upon the further experience of the race to reedit and revise them. They are not final and unchangeable truth, for there is no science so perfect that it is not subject to improvement.

What then is the relation of theory to practice ? The answer must be that theory or thinking grew out of practice; that problems came out of doing; that if doing could go on smoothly and unfailingly, without any jolts or jars, there would be no problems and no mental straining to solve them. Doing would automatically reach its goal, and thinking or theorizing would be wholly uncalled for. What reason could it possibly have for existing ? It would be the merest of shadows | an ineffective epiphe- nomenon in a universe in which everything else makes a difference and, because it does, is real.

Percepts come from doings. Knowledge, then, is not an adventitious thing. It has no being for itself.It grew out of defeated purpose, it exists to redeem action. By purpose only can it be generated, and purposive action alone will correct its defects and make it grow beyond its present stature. This means that the race as well as every individual in it is leading the experimental life. No one of them can get wisdom by merely being receptive. Even sensations do not come to us of themselves, but are internally aroused by the bodily defeats which we suffer. The suit that fits does not feel. The one that feels impedes. I can walk on the ground and hardly know that I am walking, but in walking a plank high up in the air a thousand sensations that I never noticed before make themselves felt. Sensation is due to the breakdown of habit, to the buckling up of action. The very word *perception* indicates that it is fundamentally not a receiving but a taking, an outreaching, a seizing. Why was it that the Greeks did not discover the world of physical forces, gravitation, steam, electricity, radium, and the gas engine ? Their world was like ours, these forces were working all about them. Their senses were as keen as ours. Their curiosity was as great, and as for their talent, Mr. Galton has declared " that the average ability of the Athenian race was on the lowest possible estimate very nearly two grades higher than our own [the English], that is, about as much as our raceis above the African negro." If the forces were there and the keenness of intelligence to discern them was there, why were they not found out ? The answer must be that the discovery of facts is not due to their presence nor to the possession of a mind capable of grasping them, but rather to the using of mind in the direction in which the facts lie. The Greeks were not looking for the forces of physical nature I that is why they did not see them. Inventions and discoveries are remarkably simple after they have been made, but it is only the person who is hunting for something of that sort who makes them.

One who would learn anything must put himself in the way of learning it. He must do that which will make him feel the problem. If he once gets that, his mind will work out the answer; but if he goes about getting answers to questions which he has never asked and solutions for problems which he has never raised, he will be performing only lip service to knowledge, and instead of fitting himself by getting a rich and full experience and ordering it to go on mastering experience and to help others to do so, he will be engaged in unfitting himself and in unfitting those who give and take with him.

The function of the teacher. The wise teacher is immensely helpful in this process of learning, but his influence must all be indirect like thegardener's. If I want to learn to swim, someone must show me what the best strokes are and stand by and tell me whether I am succeeding in moving my arms and legs in the way he has done, as I try to take these strokes in the air. Even if he tells me that I am succeeding, I have as yet done nothing which deserves to be called learning to swim. I cannot possibly develop the method in one medium and apply it with any degree of success in another. I can only get a merest beginning of the idea of what must be done by striking out in the air, and then I must get into the water and practice the stroke persistently for many days in the very medium in which it can be made to accomplish my purpose. It is the same stroke in both cases, but the difference between the air and the water is so great that it will not carry over to any considerable extent. The new sensations which I get when I leap into the water are so disconcerting that the old reaction is nearly unavailable in controlling them. I must, as it were, begin all over again. The teacher is still of the greatest value to me. He tells me what I must do, and he can see whether I do it or not, whereas my eyes are in the water and my attention is upon other things. He keeps me at my task; and just because he surrounds me with the necessity of trying to do the thing in what his experience has taught him isa good way, and keeps me at it and hopeful that I will learn, in time I may learn to swim.

How very different is his procedure from that of my regular teacher in school or college! In learning to swim I know from the first what it is that I want to do. I also know that I must myself do it. My teacher knows that he can help me, but he also knows that he can help me only a very little, and he does not for a moment make the mistake of supposing that any amount of verbal knowledge which he may try to give me about swimming, or any body of directions which I may strive to master in the air, will take the place of long-continued practice in the water. To the water, then, I must go, though he goes with me to help me find out what to do and to see that I do it.

Should verbal study be allowed to take the place of doing? Suppose the master workman in the shop, which is the world, should say to his apprentices: "It is true that you have come here to learn how to use the best of these tools in the working of iron, but that is a tedious and illiberal process. It will be more profitable to you if I should tell you some of the more important facts about them, and then we will spend the remainder of the time that you are to be here in analyzing the language which I shall have been compelled to employ in describing them to you. After all, language is the- mostimportant of human concerns. Some say it is a tool just like all these others here, but I think it is so much more than that that I am convinced that if you will only take the trouble, not indeed to learn to use it I for that is the least important thing about it I but to learn all the curious facts and distinctions that subtle minds have found out about it, and to recognize them when you meet instances of them, you will be better prepared to use both it and all these other tools than any amount of working with them under my direction could make you." Was it not Gorgias, the sophist, who said that rhetoric was so superior an art that if anyone wants to learn anything, say medicine, or the use of weapons, or philosophy, he should not study them but should study rhetoric instead in order to learn them? Our master workman has turned sophist and is unduly neglecting the efforts which Socrates, Plato, and Aristotle made to persuade the Athenians to a better way of thinking. His apprentices are there to learn the major arts by which "experience has taught men to make their days proceed " rather than "by chance." They have not come to acquire a knowledge *about them* merely, so that they may appreciate something of their significance when they see others employ them. They want if possible to learn at least the beginnings of their use for themselves. It is not the lore of highlyspecialized scholarship, whatever that may mean, that they seek, but such a mastery of the elements of a process which the race has found indispensable that they may practice it in an unspecialized way for themselves. Has their teacher any right to confine them to a merely descriptive acquaintance with these tools or to a dismembering of languages ?

Does each study require the pupil to learn to perform its particular kind of doing? There is a definite something to be done by the pupil when he learns to read, to write, or to number. Is there not an equally definite something to be done by him when he studies history, geography, science, language, or literature ? Merely to amass knowledge, we have seen, cannot be the object of his striving. There is far too much of it, and it is of all possible degrees of worth. There must be a principle of selection by which that which is most worth while is picked out from that which is less worth while. It is only the knowledge which works that the race cares for. It is that kind only which it is bent upon preserving. Science is a craft I literature, a *rune.* Language is to the mind what the abacus is to the Chinese merchant I a tool pure and simple. Logic and mathematics are special forms of thinking. Geography is each one's mental picture of the world. Their principles, their facts, their beauty, exist solely to be recreated byus in terms of our own conviction because they are useful, nay even indispensable, to us in steering a truly human course through life. Shall we then attempt to take them over without paying for them by the doing which alone will make us possessors of them ? Shall we try to get profit from them by dislocating their facts from their meanings and taking the facts only? Or shall we study language as a tool, science as a craft, literature as a rune, and thinking as a practice ? Here are definite things to be done I things as definite and as instrumental as reading, writing, and numbering. We must remember that doing is mental as well as manual.

The knowledge which each science offers is a body of hypothetical directions. Our argument has proceeded on the assumption that knowledge is not an end in itself but a means for the rectification of experience; that it is a body of practical directions which we must follow if we want to attain certain results. It takes the form of a hypothetical injunction: "if you want to make pig iron, treat your ore together with this fuel and this limestone flux "; " if you want to be a citizen of the United States, remember that the principles upon which the men who made it organized your government are as follows "; " if you want to be a good man, you must not forget that the ethical judgment is due to reflection upon conduct." When expanded,the scientific statement reveals its directive character. It seems to have nothing of the guideboard in it as long as it reads: " pig iron is a combination of iron with from 2 to 4.75 per cent of carbon, existing partly in a state of chemical combination with the iron and partially as mechanically distributed uncombined or graphitic carbon"; or "the declaration of principles upon which the government of the United States was founded reads as follows "; or " the ethical judgment is one whose content is conduct." Knowledge has been reported in the third person so long that it has almost lost its real character of a message to the reader. It has gained the abstractness of impersonality, but in freeing itself from prejudice and private desire it has almost lost its meaning.

Should we strive for knowledge for the sake of knowledge? Is there room for any doubt about its practical character? Yes, it would seem there is, for there is a well-worn maxim which presidents of colleges and teachers of conventionally valued studies are continually dinning into the ears of students to the effect that " knowledge exists for its own sake. The true student seeks knowledge for the sole reason that it is knowledge." As a final philosophy, this doctrine can have little meaning. As a generalization from history, it is not warranted by facts, and when tried by the test of psychologyit necessitates the severance of intelligence from action or volition. It cannot be true.

What has happened is that a counsel as to method of procedure to be followed in the getting of knowledge has been expanded into a philosophy as to its meaning. The attention of the investigator must not be diverted from the investigation which he has in hand either to count its cost or to count its probable income. .A mind divided against itself cannot observe accurately or devote itself to such patient waiting upon the facts as they demand before they will disclose themselves. Singleness of purpose is requisite. Since the purpose of the investigator is knowledge, it must be his sole aim. But when the facts are discovered, they must be tried out by another attitude. They pass out of the hands of the investigator into the hands of his fellow men. They may accept his discovery, but they ask now not, Is it so ? but What does it signify to our purposes ? What is it worth ? If the discoverer replies, " This is knowledge and you must consider it just because it is so," they reply quite scornfully that many things are so which are of no concern to them, that it is not truth but the truth which must be taken account of that they care for. And they are right. If we were pure intelligences only, knowing would be our sole concern; but we are life conservers instead, which means that the willto live selects the forms of knowing which are vital, and as soon as it can rectify the tendency of mind to delusion, it discards the rest.

Why " knowledge for tJte sake of knowledge " has become a slogan of the schools. But there is a special reason why " knowledge for the sake of knowledge " has become a slogan of the schools and is more than a methodological motto to them. It is not that the investigator must keep from confusing himself by attempting to determine the question of utility before he has found out what it is which may or may not be useful, and in so doing has deserted his function to busy himself with passing a final judgment, which is the function of society as a whole and one which] it can perform only when he has found what the facts are. It is that it is so much easier to repeat the teaching of the day before that old studies and teaching habits have a peculiar sense of fitness, and rather than discard them after their utility has gone out of them, because the conditions in which they functioned have quite changed, we take the course of least resistance and develop a bad philosophy to justify the inertia which retains them. But to do so we make our students suffer and ourselves become blind leaders of the blind.

Is all knowledge instrumental? Are all studies instrumental? Professor Keyser, in his brilliantpaper on mathematics,1 says " no." " Not in the ground of need, not in bent and painful toil, but in the deep-centred play-instinct of the world, in the joyous mood of the eternal Being, which is always young, science has her origin and root; and her spirit, which is the spirit of genius in moments of elevation, is but a sublimated form of play, the austere and lofty analogue of the kitten playing with the entangled skein or of the eaglet sporting with the mountain winds." But it must not be forgotten that there is method in this playfulness. There is the most intimate relation between play and work. Both the eaglet and the kitten, as they play, are rehearsing their ancestors' work and getting ready for their own. If the same is not true of the human playfulness which Professor Keyser is convinced that science is, why do the activities of this play stick so close to the interests which we define as work ? To be sure science is exploratory. It endeavors to run ahead of human need and to anticipate its problems before they arise, to lay up a treasure of knowledge before it is called for, but that is by no means the same thing as solving puzzles just because there is nothing more serious to do. If it be said that knowledge is due to two instincts, | curiosity and self-preservation, | it must be noted that, raciallyspeaking, these are at bottom one. The eye is ever moving up and down, to the right and to the left, searching out the field before it, seeking to light upon an object of its interest. Thus curiosity, like the hunter's dog beating the bush to raise whatever game there may be for the hunter, scours the plain in the service of self-preservation. If science is held to be the product of the play spirit because, forsooth, if she were a daughter of work she would be less beautiful and holy, it need only be pointed out that all that she gains in poetical freedom by this genealogy she loses in seriousness. At any rate, there is another point of view as to her function. One of the greatest of modern thinkers, Immanuel Kant, has stated it: "I am myself a student by inclination, I feel the whole thirst for knowledge, and the covetous restlessness that demands to advance in it, and again the satisfaction of every step of progress. There was a time when I believed that all this might constitute the honor of humanity, and I despised the crowd that knows nothing. It was Rousseau who set me right. That dazzling privilege disappeared, and I should think myself far less useful than common artisans, if I did not believe that my line of study might impart value to all others in the way of establishing the rights of humanity." 1

1 Cassius J. Keyser, Mathematics. The Columbia University Press, 1907.

1 Kant, Werke, 8, p. 624. Hartenstein.

What should education attempt to do ? Now if education should leave off its " inveterate human trick of turning names into things," give over its word worship, and ask what can I do for all these hopeful young people who trust their lives to me, what form should the answer take? This, I think. One cannot walk for another, speak for another, or digest for another. No more can he feel for another, have problems for another, think for another, or be wise or good for another. Education in the last analysis is a peculiarly personal affair. It has to do almost wholly with the man within. From the objective standpoint it is the process in which the young, surrounded by specially prepared opportunities, make their own knowledge and their own conduct each for himself. Since knowledge and conduct are but the two parts of the same sensory-motor arc, what they themselves do makes their knowledge, and this knowledge again shapes their conduct, which again brings further knowledge and is followed by correspondingly enlarged conduct. This reciprocal relation constitutes the warp and the woof of their ever-weaving experience. As it is with them, so it has been with the race since the beginning. From its doings the race has learned, and by its learning its doings have been reshaped. By many times taking the wrong road and sometimes the right one, it has accumulated a kind ofgeography of life which it puts at the service of the new travelers who are setting out upon the journey. As each one of them must choose the course he will take and as each one will choose a course which is different from that of his fellows, these directions are not put in the imperative form,| " Take this baggage and march ten parasangs to the west, then four to the south, and you will come to the city of Delight," | but are stated declara- tively, |" Two and two make four," " Blankets keep out the cold," " The very principle of ethics lies in the effort to think well." Though these things are not said in the imperative form, there is no value in saying them unless those to whom they are addressed hear them, feel their force, and shape their conduct accordingly. They are indeed hypothetical injunctions, carefully tested systems of advice worked out by our elders in the hope that we will use them. They do not ask us merely to acknowledge the existence of their experience, but to feel it and, having an inward persuasion of its force, to use it.

Now of all this stored-up experience of the race, some parts are so indispensable that all must learn to use them no matter what the particular form their lives may take. These are the elementary doings of the race | using language, reading, writing, numbering, building up a notion of the spacerelations in which men exist, and of the time relations which have conditioned and limited them and those who went before them, and learning how to live with their fellows by both outer and self- imposed control. Every one of these elementary subjects is a doing on the part of the student. The so-called higher courses of the secondary school, the college, and the university are only further doings, longer apprenticeships undertaken for a more complete mastery of these same racial tools. Having acquired some degree of skill in using these tools which all must use, the student goes in most cases from the elementary school, in some from the high school, and in a few from the college, either to the trade school or into an apprentice grade in life to acquire a special degree of skill in performing the work of some one occupation, the product of which has an exchange value. But doing is no less his object in the case of the fundamental arts than in the case of the trade which he learns. When I was a student in the law school, the professor used to say: " Our object is not to teach you the law so that you will know it. There is far too much of it for that. Our task is simply to help you to learn how to find it." So is that of the teacher of reading, spelling, numbering, history, literature, science, and philosophy. We cannot be taught any of these subjects in their completeness.In fact no one of them is complete, but we can be given such a familiarity with them that we shall find them indispensable henceforth and by means of this familiarity with them go on finding them out for ourselves as the need for them arises.

Even culture is a doing. "Culture or education is, as we may thus conclude," says Hegel, " in its ultimate sense a liberation, and that of a high kind. Its task is to make possible the infinitely subjective substantiality of the ethical life. ... In the individual agent this liberation involves a struggle against mere subjectivity, immediate desire, subjective vanity, and capricious liking. The hardness of the task is in part the cause of the disfavor under which it falls. None the less it is through the labor of education that the subjective will wins possession of the objectivity, in which alone it is able and worthy to be the embodiment of the idea."1 And again: "Culture is certainly an indefinite expression. It has, however, this meaning, that what free thought is to attain must come out of itself and be personal conviction; it is then no longer believed but investigated. ... In culture it is requisite that men should be acquainted with the universal points of view which belong to a transaction, event, etc., that this point of view, and thereby the thing, should be grasped in a universalway, in order to afford a present knowledge of what is in question. A judge knows the various laws, that is, the various legal points of view under which a thing is to be considered. ... A man of culture thus knows how to say something of everything, to find points of view in all."1

1 Hegel, Philosophy of Right (Dyde's translation), sect. 187 note. 1 Hegel, History of Philosophy, Vol. I, p. 356. London, 1892.

Education, then, is the process by which the learner in his own person comes to take the universal points of view and begins by their aid to investigate his experience and to shape it to fit his need. The circle of knowledge through which he is led to the universal viewpoints by which the race has found it profitable to take and organize its experience of inorganic and organic nature, and the thinking, willing, and aesthetic activity of the human spirit, is but a guide to help him to exercise this same mastery for himself.

7

SECTION 7

CHAPTER VII
THE PLACE OF METHOD IN EDUCATION

Comprehensibility a test of knowledge. Professor Keyser begins his illuminating discussion of mathematics 1 by citing the conviction of the French mathematician, Gergonne, that a given scientific theory cannot be said to have been perfected until it is comprehensible to the man in the street. Plato seems to have reached this same conclusion, for he regarded dialectic as the coping stone of the sciences and described it as the art of asking and answering questions; and in the " Theastetus " he made Socrates say: "And is it not shameless when we do not know what knowledge is, to be explaining the verb, ' to know' ? The truth is, Theaetetus, that we have long been infected with logical impurity. Thousands of times, have we repeated the words 'we know" and 'do not know' and 'we have or have not science or knowledge,' as if we could understand what we are saying to one another, so long as we remain ignorant about knowledge; and at this moment we are using thewords ' we understand,' ' we are ignorant,' as though we could still employ them when deprived of knowledge or science.

1 Cassius J. Keyser, Mathematics. The Columbia University Press, 1907.

" Thetetus. But if you avoid these expressions, Socrates, how will you ever argue at all ?

" Socrates. I could not, being the man I am. The case would be different if I were a true hero of dialectic; and O that such an one were present! for he would have told us to avoid the use of these terms; and at the same time he would not have spared in you and me the faults which I have noted."

Dialectic, then, or the art of asking and answering questions, is the process of stripping the verbal mask from truth and producing conviction unob- scured by language in the mind of the inquirer. To so thoroughly convince himself that his words will indubitably generate a similar conviction in others is the task of the " true hero of dialectic." There are a number of terms to be made comprehensible before education can be such a science.

The importance of method. If education is the growth of the kingdom which is within, not the communication of dogma from without but a constant appeal to the inner reference of feeling, thought, and action, the method to be employed would seem to be the most important of all the considerations which attach to it. Like true religionand undefiled it calls for something more than lip service in the temple of knowledge, something more than the memorizing of words or even of the thoughts of other men. If the only real education is the self-education of the student, how he is taught science, literature, languages, history, mathematics, and even the three fundamental arts makes all the difference between real education and make-believe, which is a great deal worse than no education at all. It is not hard for anyone who will consider these things seriously for a moment to convince himself that geometry, for example, may be the most fruitful of studies or the most empty of comprehension on the part of the learner, depending wholly upon the standpoint from which he approaches it. Mr. Herbert Spencer dared to " doubt if one boy in five hundred . . . knows his Euclid otherwise than by rote." Does the proposition read the other way to-day ? Yet mathematicians have pointed out that it is no more profitable or educative to commit the theorems and demonstrations of geometry than it is to commit the names in the city directory. Has our teaching of science, from which so much was expected, engendered the scientific mood in our students ? Does it lead to a scientific habit of mind ? Do those who pursue it acquire scientific method and learn to systematize knowledge, or dothey instead merely learn a few facts which have been systematized ? Professor Mann has declared his conviction that better results will not come from the teaching of physics until its teachers have a better philosophy of the teaching of that subject and in a recent number of *Science* l he has indicated quite clearly what he means by that.

Take the venerable subject of Latin, which in the days of its larger functioning furnished such profitable opportunities to be active-minded to the students who pursued it. It is my duty to see a good deal of high-school instruction, and what I have seen of the teaching of this study is not reassuring. I once entered a classroom while the class was engaged upon that passage of the oration for Archias in which Cicero attempts to make the thoughts of his auditors rise to the nature of the poet's mission. To do so he refers to " our Ennius," the author of the " Annals," the father of Latin poetry, "who calls the poets holy, for they seem, as it were, to be approved to us by a special gift and favor of the gods." This is a tremendous saying, and I waited with eagerness to hear what sort of a question the teacher would ask on such a passage. It came, " Why is *videantur* in the subjunctive mood ?" I visited another classroom in another school while the class was reading thefourteenth chapter of that first book, in which Caesar tells of a conference which the German chieftain Divico and his retainers attended and how Caesar addressed them, urging them to be peaceable and to send him hostages as a guaranty that they would be. Whereat the German chieftain arose and gave expression to but one sentiment, " Our fathers have taught us to receive and not to give hostages," and with that broke up the conference. I waited intently for the question that the teacher would ask, for from that German love of liberty which would not submit to be crushed out by mighty Rome herself, much that we hold dear has come down to us, and there in that remote forest two majestic conflicting forces in civilization faced each other for a moment and expressed their opposing ideals; and the question came, What mood follows &'? I went into still another classroom in still another school where students who were just beginning their study of the Latin grammar were engaged in writing a synopsis of the verb upon the blackboard. All went well until one student committed the mistake of attempting to write a perfect imperative, that disturbed the peace of the occasion. When the teacher saw it her reproof took the form: " You know that there is no such form in the book. You must follow your authority. Watch it closely and don't let thishappen again." There was no calling attention to the impossibility of giving an order to-day and having it carried out yesterday. Like Mr. Spencer's committing of geometry and Professor Mann's verbal repeating of the definitions of physics, what I have seen in many places leads me to believe that these are examples of the typical teaching of Latin. They tend to convince one that we get poor results because we do not go after better ones. *Methods are wrong because purposes are not clear.* It is much the same in the elementary schools. We teach our pupils a kind of word sounding which we call reading, but we do not often teach them to read. We teach them letter shaping, but we do not see that they carry the process into effect in their compositions and examination books, and we usually give up instructing them in handwriting before adolescence has changed their penmanship, very much as it changes the voice. They spend weary hours in performing processes in arithmetic which no longer find their counterpart in business calculations, and much of that which is taught them which is usable is put in such an abstract form that when the occasion for its use arises it is unrecognizable by them. We teach a schoolroom manipulation of language, called grammar, but it does not seem to function beyond the schoolroom. Our geography tends to be an exercise with very confusing anddifficult names, while history is a dry study which students commonly get by heart. The defects which we have noted in the teaching of geometry, physics, and Latin are to be found also in the teaching of English, modern languages, chemistry, and in most of the other studies of the secondary school and the college. Either we have been aiming at the wrong results or we have not aimed carefully enough to hit what we are aiming at. Only a pro- founder study of the method which education must employ in order to be education will tell us what the results are which we should be aiming at and how we should set about getting them. This word, *method,* has come into undeserved disrepute because it has been used to designate the rule-of- thumb devices and the teaching tricks with which badly conducted normal schools have sought to equip their students for the work of teaching. But it is much too significant a term to be harmed by such association for any but the thoughtless.

1 *Science,* March 7, 1913.

What is educational method? Method is a somewhat formidable word but its meaning is very simple | it is always a way of going to work to get certain results which we want. What we want to do determines how we shall go at it, so in order that one may go at anything methodically he must first determine what he wants to do. That is his aim, his purpose, or his undertaking. It is onlywhen he has found out quite definitely what he wants to do that he is ready to consider methods of doing it. When one knows that he wants to go to Chicago, he must next pick out the route and the train. When one knows what kind of a house he wants to build, he is ready to have a detailed plan made, and after that to employ a contractor or a carpenter to construct it for him. Method is nothing more nor less than the orderly routine to be followed in seeking to accomplish definite results. It is an outline of the steps to be taken, a plan indicating what we must do first, and what next, and what after that. Everyday speech has words and phrases for many different kinds of methods. Men talk as though there were one way of setting to work to build a house, another way of preparing to fight a battle, another way to go about governing a city, and other ways of going to work to make experiments, teach children, study lessons, etc. The fact is that all of these things call for much the same sort of planning. First the person who would do them must determine what he is setting out to do. Next he must collect the materials which are available for his purpose. Then he must allow his materials to redefine his purpose, for when he gets them together he usually finds that they will not permit him to do just what he originally planned, that is, they set a new problem very much more concreteand definite than that with which he started, and frequently they give it a quite unexpected turn. He must now proceed to work out this new problem and shape or formulate his results. These are the stages, or steps, in what is called scientific method. It is nothing mysterious, but an orderly, or systematic, way of going to work with any subject matter whatever. Scientists with almost one accord, claiming no special property in it, have insisted that men should use it in all their undertakings. They declare that the first step in any conscious process is to find out what is to be done, that the second step is to examine one's materials, that the third step is to decide what they seem to tell him, to organize them tentatively, that the fourth step is to find out if this thought of them will stand the test, and that the fifth step is to act accordingly. Educational method, like scientific method in general, is nothing more nor less than a systematic consideration of the task which education undertakes in the conviction that nothing short of such an investigation will lay bare its real purposes and the steps which are to be taken. A methodic examination of its work classifies it under the two great headings " ends " and " means." It assumes that an undertaking which takes so many of the years of the young, so much of the wealth of the land, and which makes so vast a differenceto the future is much too serious to be shaped by the dead hand of tradition or by unexamined opinions, no matter who may hold them. So responsible a task requires study. But through a strange perversity Plato's warning, that the ills of mankind cannot be expected to cease until the thinker becomes the director of human affairs, has hardly been more completely disregarded in any calling than in education. Our makers of educational opinion have employed the doctrine of formal discipline to justify themselves with a vengeance. Before assuming educational leadership, they found it necessary to make themselves expert in the work of their several callings and have trusted to that specialized expertness in some mysterious way to qualify them as authorities upon education. Under their guidance education has become institutionalized, repeating its virtues of the days before, and its vices, too, for not many of those who direct it have been trained to expertness in it.

Yet surely the education of the young is not so light a thing that a man has but to wish for knowledge about it to have it. If " the art of shaping human powers and fitting them to social uses" 1 is "the supreme art," it assuredly calls for the best and not the most indifferent of artists. No one nowadays thinks of offering himself as an authorityin medicine who has not taken pains to study medicine, yet the art of education is more difficult than that of medicine. To be sure, medicine now has a respectable body of tested, conceptualized experiences which everyone who would practice it must assimilate before he is allowed to begin, but education, too, is not without its tested experiences which should be consulted by everyone who professes to follow its calling seriously. These two sciences have much in common; they are both clearly practical. Both borrow heavily from other sciences; yet neither is content to take these contributions without reshaping them to its own use. In each a definite organizing principle determines what must be undertaken and what is pertinent. This is only another way of saying that method is the chief concern of each of them.

1 John Dewey, My Educational Creed.

What method must do.   Method must determine the course of the educational journey, for if it is indifferent how one shall travel, it is indifferent whether one shall go at all. Everyone knows in a general way what that is. There is the individual, on the one hand, and the world in which he must live, on the other. Men have been living here a long time and have accumulated a great deal of knowledge which somehow or other must guide each new traveler. But how shall these two terms of the educational equation be brought together?Just what is the result which we seek? Again, what parts of this knowledge shall we make the child take account of ? There is a lot of it I some of it is vastly important and some is not. Is there any principle by which we may select it ? Does it make any difference what kind of a mind the learner has?

. His own doing must be directed to the doing of those acts which the race has found indispensable to its well-being. Science, religion, literature, government must be born again in him. That part of the directive knowledge which the race puts at his disposal which he can use, he must master not statically but dynamically. Not all that passes for knowledge is directive, but unless it works it is not knowledge. So out with that part of it which belongs only to erudition or with that large part which is professional only to the scholar. The student need not concern himself with that until he begins to prepare for the special calling to which it pertains. The land which is common to untechnical pursuits is, however, vast in extent. He must preempt no more of it than he can till. It is uneconomical for society to allow him to claim title to more of this field than he can make produce.

The aim of education. But what kind of a crop must he grow? A social crop. Education is to make him into a social factor. " Pedagogy," saysHegel, " is the art of making men ethical. It looks upon man as natural and points out the way in which he is to be born again. His first nature must be converted into a second spiritual nature in such a manner that the spiritual becomes in him a habit."1 The particular must be universalized. One's private instincts, desires, emotions, thoughts, and deeds must be rationalized. His instincts must be socialized, his desires must be civilized, his emotions must learn to love and hate aright, his thoughts must be ordered, and in his deeds it must be not his private self but the good which worketh. In other words, he must learn to do as he would be done by, think from the standpoint of the race, "have sound social feeling if his doings are to be deeds, not misdeeds," make his desires wholesome, and regulate his instincts to social ends. In short, he must become a person. This we are told is the highest aim of man. Individuality is only its possibility. It is not until the individual learns to want what God wants, to will the will of God, that he becomes free. "The very essence of personality is our implicit or explicit identification of ourselves with some particular traits of mind, for the weakest personality is that which possesses no particular psychical traits at all." The development of personality, then, is the object of education. And thisdevelopment consists in the conscious building up within the learner of certain racially useful traits of mind. He must direct his will to their attainment. He must make himself the owner of the personality which he would have. Though social achievement furnishes the model, he himself must paint the picture. The origin of the word is significant of the method by which personality is acquired. It comes from the Latin *personare,* meaning " to sound through," and referring to the actor's habit of speaking through a mask. A personality is the result of personating. To put on Christian personality means to personate a Christian ; to put on moral personality, to personate a moral man; to put on intellectual personality, to personate an intellectual man. In the Roman law a person is a human being invested with legal rights and liable for the performance of corresponding duties, a being who can do and does certain things. Therefore a child, an insane person, or a slave, who could not under the law perform these acts, were not persons. The individual puts on personality by personating or identifying himself with the preferred traits of the species. Though an individual he learns to live the life of his kind. By this personating of the social part, individuality is transformed into personality.

1 Hegel (Dyde's translation), Philosophy of Right, 151.

If this inwrought personality is our ideal of education, must not all that is learned be inwrought in order that this may be its culmination ? We cannot strive for an autonomy of conscience without an autonomy of consciousness. The moral personality is only the mental personality functioning in one direction. It is the mental personality that we must seek to develop, and it can be brought to being only by the individual identifying himself with, or making his own, certain specific social traits of mind. When we speak of a moral personality we intend to refer to the fact that the person who has developed it has made his instincts and desires to act under all circumstances in certain systematic ways. When we speak of a mental personality we intend to refer to a similar achievement in mental organization, to the fact that capacities have learned to work in socially approved, specifically useful ways. The man with a trained body is one who has learned both how to use it and to use it to accomplish certain social ends, such as health, work, pleasure, self- defense. He has wrought out for himself a certain physical attitude or temper and can be depended upon to act regularly according to it. The man whom we think of as a moral personality has established no less definitely organized moral reactions. He has certain traits of character. We say of such an one we always know where to find him. He hasidentified himself with a specific type of conduct. Through all the shifts of circumstance he preserves a steady demeanor, maintaining in the midst of trials and temptations the right opinion of things to be feared and not to be feared, for the man within him has chosen to value and to do in these ways. Just so the mental personality has learned specific methods of attack, of deliberating, of searching, of conjecturing, of trying out his conjectures, and of formulating his conclusions. He does not differ from other men in the things which concern him, for human interests are common to us all; but he does differ from them in the way he goes to workl in that he converts his experience into questions or problems which he does not dismiss with a word, but toward which he maintains the suspended judgment, ceaselessly collecting information which has a bearing upon them and, in the light of what he finds, recasting his problem and testing what seems to be the answer until he is quite sure that he has reached it. " The typically scientific mind may be described as one which stands in a definite relation to as-yet-unknown Truth, and especially to that portion of the as-yet-unknown which is just below the horizon of knowledge," says Mrs. Boole. "In proportion as a mind is non-scientific, the occurrence of an unfamiliar phenomenon stimulates it to form some immediate classification or judgment.A new statement is hailed at once as ' true' or ' false '; a new fact is classified as ' good' or ' bad,' 1 nice ' or ' nasty'; an unfamiliar action is ' right' or 'wrong.' In proportion as a mind is scientific, the occurrence of a new phenomenon tends to set it vibrating with a consciousness of coming revelation and to start a certain cycle of mental attitudes, a cycle of the following kind, homage, attention, observation, analysis, antithesis, synthesis, contemplation, effacement, repose, judgment or classification. The cycle varies in duration; each phase may occupy a few seconds or many months, or even years; but the tendency to fall into some such sequence as that above described at the touch of a new fact is what constitutes the essentially scientific condition."1

The mental personality is one which has learned to work in a certain effective way. Like the physical or the moral, it is an inwrought mode of action. How can it be developed? Professor Thomson italicizes his answer, " *The scientific temper must be wrought out by each one for himself.*"2

It is of much more importance that one should develop the scientific mood than that he should amass the facts of chemistry, physics, or biology,and it is of very much more importance that one should develop the emotional mood than that he should know all that there is to be known *about* the poetry of Shelley or Shakespeare.

1 M. E. Boole, Preparation of the Child for Science, p. 15. The Clarendon Press, 1904.

1 Thomson, Introduction to Science, p. 33. Home University Library.

Superiority of "knowledge of" to "knowledge about" If the organizing of this kind of a personality within himself on the part of each student is the aim of education,

Professor James's distinction between the two kinds of knowledge is vitally important. It is the knowledge *of* science, languages, literature, history, mathematics, philosophy, and the other socially profitable ways of dealing with human experience which we must strive for, for while knowledge *of* them requires knowledge *about* them, knowledge *about* them does not necessarily include knowledge *of* them. Pine wood is a social fact of importance perhaps to everyone at some time or other in his existence. One may know a great deal *about* it, but only the boy who has split it and broken it into kindling lengths, who has planed it and sawed it, has a knowledge *of* it. Just so, it is one thing to know *about* English and quite another thing to know it. The same is true of French or geography or physics, indeed of every subject which we study. Knowledge is personal, it is the identification of the self with the traits of experience which they present. And knowledge *of* them every student can have if his teacher hasbut once considered its superiority to knowledge *about* them and has organized his work to make it possible. But, it will be said, to *get* a knowledge of pine is easy since one can take it into his own hands and manipulate it to his own purposes, while one cannot take history or geography into his own hands and manipulate them. Not so. It is just as easy to work with literature or history or geography as it is with pine wood. The working is no less working because in the case of the pine wood there is a larger manual element than in the other. It is mental working that the race chiefly values, and that each student may learn to perform it in a satisfactory manner for himself is the reason for his being sent to school. It is easy to see that when he studies reading, writing, and arithmetic it is what he learns to do that concerns us. It is not so clear that when he studies history our chief aim is to train him to historize, or geography to geogra- phize, or geology to geologize. Yet, as we have seen, these several studies are only ways in which the race has learned to handle its experience, and our study of them is a challenge to us to begin handling our experience in their ways. It may seem that it is much easier to identify oneself with that racially profitable trait which is the practice of numbering and calculating than with those other racially profitable traits which we have calledhistorizing or geographizing, because when we study arithmetic we ourselves solve problems and come to think of ourselves as problem solvers while in history or geography we only take instead of doing. That is due to the way we teach these studies, not to the studies themselves. They come to us just as the pine wood does I as something given. They challenge us to work with them, to ask questions of them, to search in them for the answers to our own questions, to rearrange their material, to learn to handle their concepts, to make our own generalizations, and then to try them out for ourselves. When one studies history he does so in order to make his own historic interpretation, to construct his own outline of the way events have succeeded events in time; when geography, to make his own picture of the way the conditions of human life affect each other in space. He learns to think historically and to think geographically. Just so, " poetry," we are told, " exists only in the reflective consciousness."1 " The poem, like the picture and the sonata, is no copy of nature; its appeal is to the imagination which is contemplative, and not to that which is merely reproductive."2 To study them one must use his own mind, and every science as well as every art seems to have that same challenge tous as its chief reason for existing. If it could speak it would say to us, " Learn how to handle my subject matter, learn how to work with my concepts, see if you can frame questions like those which the man who shaped me framed, see if you can search out their answers, see if you can organize and reorganize my material and solve problems with my aid."

1 Haldane, The Pathway to Reality, Vol. II, 183. New York, 1905. a Ibid. 185.

Importance of the context in connection with which processes are acquired. One cannot develop the mood by itself; he must have a content about which he may develop it. It makes a difference what that particular content is in connection with which he attempts to develop his personal system of reactions. It must not be one which makes the habitual attitudes we seek to engender in him impossible. On the other hand, it must contain plenty of middle terms or elements common to it and to the subsequent experience to which it is intended that the same methods of reaction shall be applied. For unless the new situation is recognizably identical with the old familiar one, it cannot call for a similar response. The learning which would provide methods of handling it must be kindred to it. The concepts without their normally experienced percepts are empty, and blind as well. This is perhaps the greatest fallacy of modern education, that it seeks to set up the reactionswhich it values in connection with a content which is nonrepresentative and leaves the student with the conviction that he has learned nothing that is applicable to anything outside of school. The subject matter of the course of study cannot be selected because it lends itself most readily to classroom manipulation. To choose it for that reason is to consider only the advantage of the teacher. It is not teaching which must be made easy, but learning, and to empty it of intelligible meaning which the student can lay hold of is to make it to him a vain, conventional thing. What is taught in the school is just as valuable there as it is in the world outside the school and no more valuable. It is for their world value and not for any abstract school value that studies must be selected. The content, then, makes an enormous difference to the learner in terms of interest and comprehension when he is learning, and in terms of usability in after days. Futurity is not only the great concern of mankind; it is peculiarly the concern of youth. It is toward things to come that education must face. The several disciplines are tools which the race has found it as necessary to use as the hammer, the oar, and the skinning knife. They are valuable just in so far as they serve. But institutionalized education being only a part of a whole process, that part which instructs but does not try outthe results of its instruction has cut itself away from its own corrective. One body of men teaches; another body tries out the results of their teaching. The educational producer is rarely the consumer. If he were he could be trusted, for he would apply the pragmatic test to his own work. As he is not, the sufficiency of what he does is not tested by its outcome but by the traditions which support it. As a result, education tends to remain uncritical and irrational. It does not strive for a clear comprehension of its end, and it exhibits an undue love for a merely traditional course of study.

What should be studied? The object of the course of study is undoubtedly to put at the disposal of the student that body of concepts, methods, and reports of percepts which, when made his own by use, will enable him to shape his conduct with a minimum of wasteful experimenting, in ways which the race has found to bring profitable results. Every subject in it gained its place there because of its manifest utility at the time it was admitted. But the changing universe has run away from some of the studies. They have lost their utility, but they still keep their place in the course as though they retained it. Consequently the course of study has become ritualistic I the spirit of life has, in a measure, gone out of it. If it were framed with forethought and design, would it contain just thatwhich it now contains? In this connection certain queries constantly recur to me which I find that I cannot answer. The Greek word *logos* means "word," and it also means "idea" or "thought." Why is it that education limits its interest so largely to the word and neglects the thought ? Education, we are told over and over again, is primarily linguistic. Should this be so? Was it not John Milton who said, " And though a linguist should pride himself to have all the tongues that Babel cleft the world into, yet if he have not studied the solid things in them as well as the words and lexicons, he were nothing so much to be esteemed a learned man, as any yeoman or tradesman competently wise in his mother dialect only" ? Why in place of studying the Greek grammar or even the Greek language do we not read the "solid things " in the literature of that remarkable people ? If Rome's great contribution to civilization was law and orderly administration, why does our study of Latin not undertake to lead us to some knowledge of the nature of Rome's greatest gift to the world ? Why instead of confining our students to English literature do we not first make them acquainted with the first-class literature of mankind? Is there any really good and sufficient reason why the student in the general courses should not know his Homer, his Plato, his Dante, and Cervantes as wellas his Shakespeare ? Why in place of the more remote aspects of mathematics do not such homely and commonly used matters as the theory and practice of statistics, graphs, simple projective geometry, and mechanical drawing come in for general attention? Why do we not give as much attention to physical training as the Greeks did? We know that it is more necessary than they did, and we know more about scientific ways of instructing in it. Why do we not teach each person the elements of health protection ? Why, though we say that the object of education is preparation for intelligent citizenship, do we not teach each person the elements of law ? Why, when we say that the object of education is morality, do we trust to incidental and indirect instruction to generate clear notions of what morality is ? Why, when we say that one of our chief objects is to teach scientific method, do we not from his very beginning in the elementary school involve each student in a critical search for the reasons for common things ? Why when we study the languages, do we not learn to use them ? Why is not everyone taught shorthand, typewriting, and the elements of accounting? Why is it not part of our theory of general education to teach everyone a trade, as Locke and Rousseau recommended ? Why do we not teach every student how to study ?

Fitting studies to students. But the course of study is not the only feature of education which calls for the application of method; the selection of the students who should be allowed to pursue the several studies is no less important. " Not more than half the students in my class in geometry could study the subject otherwise than by rote," says a very skillful teacher. " What am I to do with the others ?" Custom says, " Teach them by rote and give them a passing mark at the end of the term "; but custom is not critical. Is it fair to delude them or to delude ourselves into believing that they are profiting by pursuing geometry when they cannot learn it otherwise than by rote ? Assuming that these are the facts, does it not follow that we have a duty to keep them out of the geometry class and other classes in which the same thing happens, and to direct them to studies which they can pursue to advantage ? This is a large subject and one with which education is only beginning to concern itself seriously. Each one is born with natural aptitudes. Fortunately we cannot all follow the same calling. Cooperative social life is made possible by the fact that nature equipped us in some measure to be specialists. Plato, who was the first to examine education profoundly, advised the use of thoroughgoing trials and tests to determine what sort of studies each one was fitted to pursue. For himthe education which the individual required could not be decided by birth or the occupation of his father. He must himself be consulted as to his fitness, and having proved it, the state could not neglect to give him adequate opportunity. Education could not afford to be a hit-or-miss affair. There can be no doubt that he was wiser in this respect than subsequent educational practice has been. His wisdom is beginning to be put into effect. The way to proceed is by no means clear. Yet scientific methods of fitting studies to students must somehow be found.

The wise and enlightened selection of studies on the basis of their social value is one phase of education which calls for the elaboration of method. The no less wise and enlightened selection of the students whose aptitudes enable them to pursue these several studies with advantage to themselves and society is another. All this, however, though indispensable, is preliminary to the real work of teaching. When the subject has been determined and the class is there ready to begin its work, does it make any difference how the teacher proceeds ? The fact is that it does. We may spend millions in erecting school palaces; we may gather the youth of the nation together in them; we may employ an army of teachers to teach them just what they should know; but unless they are givenan opportunity to learn, the undertaking will be in vain. The test of teaching then is learning. That must be done by the students.

Methods of instruction. Two methods and their variations are open to us. Both are very old, and both are Greek in their origin. The one is the method of Pythagoras, which enjoins the student to a long and awesome silence and requires that he sit outside the veil and only listen to the master's wisdom; the other is the method of Socrates, " who spoke less than his scholars " and so wrought upon them that they discussed everything. The one is the service of the letter, which killeth; the other, the unlocking of the spirit, which is life.

The recitation method. The modern master, before whose invisible presence we learn to maintain an awesome mental silence in our early years, is the maker of the textbook. To get our lesson means to get his words by heart. What is committed in the seats is repeated in the recitation. The teacher assigns the pages and hears the lesson " said." This is the recitation method. The word is used in a special sense l a recitation is a selected bit of poetry or prose committed to memory and recited aloud, but except that it has not to do with specially selected poetry or prose, the ordinary recitation is just like the extraordinary one. I remember that when I began to study geometry, I was indoubt what was expected of me and decided at a venture to memorize the theorems which were printed in italics. When the teacher called for the proof of the theorem, I found that something more must be committed, though it seemed to me an unjust burden to put upon anyone to require him to memorize not only what someone else had found out to be true but the steps by which he had come to his conclusion. This makes a deadly dull business of studying. If drudgery, which is so forbidding that all men quite rightly seek to escape it, is work robbed of its meaning, this kind of work is drudgery, for the student sees no glimmer of meaning in it. Moreover it is equally devitalizing to the teacher, for it reduces him to a lesson-hearing machine. There are several degrees in this process. That one which employs memoriter learning most completely is called the examination method. The lesson is assigned. The pupils must prepare themselves to recite it verbatim. The teacher calls them up in turn. Each one attempts to repeat the lesson. The teacher puts down a mark in a book when he has finished and signals to the next one to proceed. It is possible in this way to hear a whole class recite without saying a word.

The ordinary recitation is a slight variation from this one. The main thing is still the repeating of the lesson, but the teacher sometimes gives a cuewhen it has been forgotten, and once in a while cross-questions the students to see if they have the proper degree of familiarity with that which they have been learning. Quiz methods and review methods are usually only more elaborate forms of the recitation. It is distinguished from every other method by the fact that the class exercise is a recitation, that is, a rehearsal of what has been learned before the class exercise takes place. There are some studies, for example, history, geography, spelling, grammar, Latin, algebra, modern languages, literature, etc. which many teachers believe admit of no other treatment. So commonly is the memoriter method employed that its prevalence has called forth the aphorism that "the German teacher teaches but the American teacher hears lessons."

The lecture method. The recitation method is widely used in elementary and secondary schools. It is used, also, in colleges and sometimes in university teaching, but the more advanced instruction is given chiefly by lectures. The verb *to lecture* means " to read." That method of instructing came into vogue in the medieval universities because books were scarce then and there was no other way in which the students might be put into possession of them so easily as by the teacher dictating their contents to them. Nowadays many lecturersread, but some discourse upon their subject from brief written notes or discuss it extempore. To lecture is exceedingly profitable to the teacher, for it involves the systematizing to a high degree of his own knowledge upon the subject. It is a skillful, attractive, dignified, exceedingly stimulating, and irresponsive method of teaching. To present matters which must be brought together from many authorities, to rearrange outlines, to formulate conclusions or submit the results of one's own investigations, perhaps, requires one to lecture. But it is a peculiarly unsuccessful method of teaching. Orators and lecturers, like books, can neither ask nor answer questions. They are monologists all.

What is spoken cannot be reperused unless it is taken down, and only a part of it can be taken down. The student must become a copyist while the lecture is proceeding. If he studies his notes afterward, he studies only fragments of what the lecturer has said. The attitude which he is invited to take, and which he gets into the habit of taking, is passive and receptive. He is there to take knowledge, not to doubt, inquire, and investigate. He is not put into a position where he must think for himself. The only thing he must do is to memorize, but " to know by heart is not to know at all."

Professor Osborn calls this " afferent, or inflowing mediaeval, and oriental kind of instruction inwhich the student is rarely if ever forced to do his own thinking, the 'centripetal system.'" He declares himself an insurgent in education, altogether opposed to the " overfeeding which stuffs, crams, pours in, spoon-feeds, and as a sort of deathbed repentance institutes creative work after graduation." He asks the students, "Is your idea of a good student that of a good ' receptacle ' ? " " You should know that not a five foot shelf of books, not even the ardent reading of a fifty foot shelf aided by prodigious memory, will give you that enviable thing called culture, because the yard stick of this precious quality is not what you take in but what you give out, and this from the subtle chemistry of your brain must have passed through a mental metabolism of your own so that you have lent something to it."1

The trouble with both the recitation and the lecture method is that they are based upon a wrong theory of knowledge. No one can make knowledge for another any more than he can breathe for another. It is no ready-made thing which can be stored up in books and handed on in lectures. Each one out of his own awareness must build his world. The raw materials of knowledge, books, lectures, laboratories, and schools may provide, butthere are subtle processes of questioning, feeling, thinking, assuming, testing, and using which each one must apply for himself in order to reduce these raw materials to essential parts of his own system.

1 Osborn/Huxley and Education, 26-28. Charles Scribner's Sons, New York, 1910.

What determines whether a method is good or bad? I think we may say that methods of teaching are good just in the degree that they make the student a partner in the enterprise of learning. If he merely sits still and listens, he learns something, but not much. If he reads his book and memorizes it, he learns more because he does more for himself. Can we not surround him with conditions which will involve him profoundly in the process of distinguishing, valuing, selecting, arranging, and using knowledge ? If the crown and fulfillment of education is the ability to do research work, at what age must the student begin the work of searching ? The notion that searching is a method which can profitably be employed only in postgraduate instruction is completely disproved by what goes on in every kindergarten in the land. The comforting thing about that method is that it can be used in some degree in the teaching of practically every subject and in every grade of instruction. It requires simply that the learner shall be allowed to discover truth for himself, that he shall be put into the way of having his own experiences, formulating his ownconcepts, and learning their meaning and how to use them by using them. How shall the student be induced to think for himself? How are the states of feeling out of which sensations and opinions arise to be generated?

The Socratic method. Fortunately the inventor and the most successful of all the users of the method, Socrates himself, has supplied the answer. Thinking " is the conversation which the soul holds with herself in considering of anything. I speak of what I scarcely understand; but the soul when thinking appears to me to be just talking I asking questions of herself and answering them, affirming and denying. And when she has arrived at a decision, either gradually or by a sudden impulse, and has at last agreed, and does not doubt, this is called her opinion. I say then that to form an opinion is to speak, and opinion is a word spoken I I mean to one's self and in silence, not aloud to another."1 But if thinking is speaking to one's self silently, does not audible speaking under conditions which do not supply the words or call for " mere conversation," but require us to hunt for what we should say, involve thinking also ? Was it not for this very reason that Socrates and Plato employed the conversational, or dialogue, method in their teaching? And wasit not that method as surely as the lofty character of the subjects which they led their students to investigate by it which made their instruction the most fruitful which has ever been given by teacher to pupil ? Their use of question and answer was due to the conviction that truth is a thing to be found out, not a thing which can be imparted. It is a singular circumstance in the history of culture that as soon as men abandoned their method and began to try to impart truth as something preestablished which has only to be handed down from teacher to student, the great age of intellectual discovery came to a close.

1 Plato, Theaetetus, 190.

TIu heuristic method. The Socratic method, then, shorn of the necessity which required the teacher of mankind at Athens to prepare the way for it by first taking the conceit out of some of the men upon whom he used it, seems to be the one which makes real teaching possible. The heuristic method, the adoption of which has been so vigorously pleaded for in recent days, is nothing but the Socratic method modernized. The essence of this method is that the pupil must be the discoverer. All that is known which he is to learn must be rediscovered by him. To teach by this method does not mean to tell, but to ask. When difficulties paralyze the learner, he may be given a cue by a suggestion or a question which willput him into action, but the teacher is there to occasion the problems, not to supply answers before questions have been raised within the learner's mind. Professor Meiklejohn contended " that the permanent and universal condition of all method in education is that it be heuristic."1 In every subject the student must do his own mental walking. The teacher may pick him up when he stumbles, and when he is lost should show him the way, but must not carry him. The method assumes that the student can think. Every kinder- gartner knows that this is true even of the smaller learners. It strives to put each student upon his own feet and to keep him from leaning unduly upon his fellows. Each individual must develop his own understanding.

The genetic method. The genetic method differs from the heuristic method in the respect that the subject is developed by the class under the guidance of the teacher. The questions are directed to the class as a whole. Each one makes an effort to answer them or asks such questions as arise in him. The teacher is a chairman presiding over a discussion. The textbook serves as an outline of topics to be considered. Every lesson is opened by a. discussion in the class, is then studied inthe textbook and in as many other books as are available, and then rediscussed in the class. Individual work, recitations, examinations, and lectures all have a place in this scheme of teaching, but the class discussion is the main thing. It converts the recitation period into a thinking period, in which each student does his best studying under the stimulus of his fellows and of the teacher. In certain subjects, say mathematics, physics, laboratory chemistry, and composition, in which the work that each one should perform for himself can be clearly indicated, the heuristic method would seem to be best, but in other subjects, like literature, languages, history, and philosophy, where the give and take from the teacher and from one's fellow students is perhaps of greater value, the genetic method is more serviceable. Learners cannot, to be sure, find out everything for themselves, but they can at any rate employ the methods of fact finding and the methods by which facts are classified and conclusions from them deduced and tried out. These methods of teaching have been sufficiently tested to warrant the conclusion that the learner learns by them, that his interest grows instead of dwindling under them, that those schools are good schools which are talking schools, and those are poorer than they should be in which thestudents merely attempt to imbibe knowledge. The school must become a workshop in which students work at definite tasks, and by their own efforts under the master's eye learn to use the great tools with which the race has by the same process learned to do its work. To give a child a conception instead of inducing him to find it seemed to the saintly Pestalozzi to be a wicked act. It robs the child of opportunity. Does it not rob society as well?

1 See Armstrong, The Teaching of Scientific Method, p. 237. London, 1910.

SECTION 8

CHAPTER VIII
LEARNING BY PROBLEM GETTING

Does mere observing teach us? How many years of sitting beside a chauffeur and watching him guide the machine must one put in before he can learn how to drive himself, if he never takes the wheel ? How many years of careful observation of the work of a carpenter will teach the trade, provided one does not take the tools into his own hands? In cities, wherever men are engaged in difficult work which can be seen from the streets, a crowd gathers to watch them. Do the persons in these crowds learn to perform the work which they observe so intently? How long would one have to watch a company of experts play tennis or baseball in order to become a qualified player himself? The answer to all of these questions is that no amount of watching of itself will enable one to do any of these things. One may grow gray as a baseball fan without learning how to catch or throw a ball; and one may ride beside a skillful chauffeur all his days without acquiring any skill in driving the machine. Mere looking and listening will not teach. To learn todrive, one must take the wheel; to learn to hammer, one must hammer; and to learn to work with concepts, one must work with concepts. So marvelously does action sharpen our looking and listening that the mere beginnings of doing, on our own part, convert our seeings and hearings into values.

The person who has tried to drive the machine learns something by watching the expert. The embryo baseball player profits by watching the game. I watch men skate and see every movement they make, but the instant I myself put on the skates, I begin to see that there is much more to skating than my observation had told me. Indeed, even the prospect of taking the wheel as soon as we come to an easy piece of road converts my desultory attention into the closest interest, and I now become all eyes and ears for what is being done.

We are motor-ideo beings. The new school of psychologists contends that, since behavior is the characteristic of living things, the only way to study consciousness is by studying behavior. Consciousness is motor ǀ every sensory state tends to become an appropriate muscular movement. Ideas produce action. We are ideo-motor beings. The inverse has been neglected, but it is equally true. We are motor-ideo beings. Action produces ideas. It is the striving to attain an end which developsknowledge. Consciousness is conative. Mind is a problem solver. It is perplexity, doubt, conflict, and not the even tenor of an untroubled mind which causes reflection. Where there is no question, there can be no searching for an answer. Where there is no problem, there is no occasion for the mind to converse with " herself." Seeings, hearings, feelings, thinkings, and doings follow each other at random. We are not concerned about anything in particular, our minds go woolgathering, we daydream. A purpose to be served, an undertaking to be accomplished, keeps the flow of ideas within bounds. What I read or heard or saw but a moment ago, while purposelessly daydreaming, flitted by in a mist, but now parts of what I read, see, or hear, which are congruent with my purpose, bite themselves into my awareness. Now I learn, for I hunt, I select, I reject, I scheme, plan, fit, and am satisfied or dissatisfied with my own state of mind. To be active minded is to be acting ǀ not taking things as they come, but making them come our way. But this is no hit-or-miss affair. We cannot think by commanding ourselves to think, neither can we feel by telling ourselves that the occasion calls for feeling. There are certain preliminaries which must be attended to before one can command his own mind. Learning to use one's own mind,however, in such ways that he will go on using it to advantage as long as he lives is the one, great, supreme object of education. Now that psychology has defined itself as the study of behavior, education must follow suit by conceiving its mission as that of training the student to profitable behavior ǀ that is, to do the things that the situations which he will meet in life call for. Our contention is that these social doings are definite responses to concrete situations, and that the learning which will fit us to make them must be the learning of definite doings, not that vague thing which is called general training. One definite reaction which all must learn is how to set about learning anything. What are the outlines of that process ?

What the psychology of attention tells us as to how to go to work. If one would thread a needle, there is one spot where he should keep his eye. If one is shooting at a mark, it will" not do to let his eyes wander up and down, looking now upon the muzzle of the gun, now upon the trigger. If one is trying to drive a nail, he should not fix his gaze upon his fingers which hold the nail, nor yet upon the hammer. Golf players who give raw beginners their preliminary lessons insist that they should fix their eyes upon a certain object. Ball players are told to keep their eyes not upon the bat, but on the ball. Boxers are taught to watchthe eyes of their antagonist. The strange thing about all this is that, if one will only keep his eyes fastened to the right spot, his muscles will do about what is required of them, whereas no amount of urging will make them respond in other than a fumbling way unless he does keep his eyes upon the proper object.

Why is this ? Why cannot one thread a needle just as well by keeping his eyes fixed upon the point of the needle as upon its eye, or drive a nail just as well by looking at the head of the hammer as by looking at the head of the nail ? The thread must be put through the eye of the needle. It must be the focus of attention in order that the coordinations may be directed to it. Of themselves they center upon it just so long as it is specially sensed. As soon as we begin to examine the sharpness of its point, its weight, its length, or other sensation aspects of it, our muscular system shapes itself to these ends. Everyone has had the experience of thinking ahead of the word he was writing to the word he meant to write next, and finding that his pen had written the word which he was thinking about, not the word which he had set it to write. If the sensation is clear enough the motor activity comes of itself. In learning to ride a bicycle or to drive an automobile, the beginner sees an object which he muststeer away from, and the next instant finds that he has steered right up to it. The sensory content sets off the motor response. To steer in the right way, one must keep his eye upon the course which he should follow, not upon the one which he must not take. This is as true in morals as it is in driving a machine. And in acquiring all forms of skill the proper focusing of attention, or looking where one should look, would seem to be much more than half the battle. Training to do anything, then, would seem to be largely a matter of learning to keep one's eye to the right spot and to let one's doings shape themselves accordingly. It is the business of sensory experience to define the problem, set the task, or locate the end. Motor responses immediately fall upon it, and in so far as habitual doings can handle it, it is already solved. If they fail to respond in the proper degree, their failure must be looked at and a try-try-again process must ensue, each new effort providing a new object to be looked at before a new and better doing is attempted. Thus even try-try-again learning is a process of redefining what must be done, and not making the first response over and over again blindly.

Where must one keep his eye in studying? If one cannot learn to shoot at a mark, or to thread a needle, or to bat a ball, without learning to keephis eye on the right spot, is it likely that he can learn to read or to write, to think geometry or logic, to use scientific method, or to make history or literature function in the life which he leads, without learning what to look for before his nervous system can make the responses which he wants it to make? Studying is conscious learning. Consciousness is conative. It exists to define problems for organic responses to close in upon and solve. When the problem is sufficiently defined, the solution seems to come of itself. I desire to learn to shoot at a mark so as to hit the bull's-eye. There is nothing which I can do but to keep redefining my aim. My nervous system will have to catch the knack of responding better and better for itself. I can only see what is wanted and trust it to comply. Everyone who has practiced a long time at anything, knows how mysteriously the skill finally comes. More and more clearly he sees what must be done, but somehow the muscles refuse to do it. Yet let him but keep on asking and re- asking them to make the response which he seeks, and one day, all of a sudden, they will supply it, if it is in their power. " It's dogged that does it," said Darwin. The mathematician who carries his problem about with him month after month, perhaps even year after year, at last sees the solution staring him in the face. He does not know justhow it came, but because he had the problem and kept the problem, it came. " Seek and ye shall find" is the law. But how can skill in shooting come to those who do not aim at the bull's-eye, but are content to discharge the gun only in its general direction? Is there any profit at all in cultivating that kind of marksmanship? It may serve a casual interest to know in a general way how the thing is done, should one ever want to do it, and what degree of skill others have attained in it, but that sort of knowledge seems so trifling and dehumanizing that one longs once more to hear the Spartan cry, " Strip or leave the gymnasium."

Setting the learner on the track of invention. " I am convinced that the method of teaching which approaches most nearly to the methods of investigation is incomparably the best"; wrote Edmund Burke, " since not content with serving up a few barren and lifeless truths, it leads to the stock on which they grew; it tends to set the learner himself on the track of invention, and to direct him into those paths in which the author has made his own discoveries."1

Let us go then to the inventors, and ask them how they found out what they did not know before, in order that we may learn the process of discovery from them. First we must note that even thegreatest of them did not create something out of nothing. " Imagination is constructive, not creative." John Ruskin points out that man with all his genius has not succeeded in creating a new kind of animal. In his most unhampered dreaming he has simply rearranged in new ways the parts of the animals which he found here. Every invention is that sort of a variation of what has been experienced. But how did men come to vary their experiences in novel and highly beneficial ways ? Did they accidentally stumble upon these variations? Did the images and thoughts with which their minds were filled by chance coagulate into new forms, so that mind, by a sort of spontaneous generation, developed new and profitable ideas ? It is not in that way that men have made inventions. Casual interest, reverie, and daydreaming do not produce discoveries. If they did, indifference would not save them. There is, to be sure, an element of accident in all invention, but the invention itself is not a lucky accident. We undertake something. That undertaking calls up remembered images, free images, and thoughts in new relations. Our effort sharpens attention. We are searching for means to ends. Our trying makes the parts of experience fall into new combinations. An unexpectedly apt variation tumbles out before us. We did not know what it might be before itdisclosed itself. It presented itself accidentally, but we were hunting for something along that line. Newton's description of his own method was that he pondered again and again on a question. " The combinatory law of the images " is not under control. Purpose brings hosts of them under the eye of attention. One after the other they are dismissed as unsatisfactory. " Suddenly that particular form arises to the light which harmonizes perfectly with the ruling idea, mood or design."1 Was its coming, then, due to chance or to the insistence of the ruling idea, mood, or design ? " The same relation that a word solving a riddle bears to that riddle is born by the modern conception of light to the facts discovered by Grimaldi, Romer, Huygens,

Newton, Malus, and Fresnel, and only by the help of this slowly developed conception is our mental vision enabled to embrace the broad domain of facts in question."2

1 Quoted in Armstrong, The Teaching of Scientific Method, p. 237.

How inventions are made. Uniquely pernicious is the popular theory as to how inventions are made, for it does irreparable damage to the minds of the young. A myth tells us that the moving teakettle lid directed James Watt to his valuable discovery. But note the genealogy of that invention. Hero of Alexandria, about 130 B.c., describeda device by which the air in a hollow altar, when heated by a fire upon it, drove water from a vessel below it into a suspended bucket, causing it to descend and open the attached temple doors. Gerbert of Aurillac (d. 1002) and Leonardo da Vinci both seem to have tried to make steam do mechanical work. Delia Porta in 1601 anticipated the steam engine which Savery a century later made. In 1663 the Marquis of Worcester proposed, if he did not indeed make, the first useful steam engine. In 1698 Savery obtained a patent for a water-raising engine. In 1705 Newcomen made the piston engine a success. In 1763 James Watt, " an instrument maker in Glasgow, while engaged by the university in repairing a model of New- comen's engine, was struck by the waste of steam to which the alternate chilling and heating of the cylinder gave rise. He saw that the remedy, in his own words, would lie in keeping the cylinder as hot as the steam which entered it. With this view he added to the engine a new organlan empty vessel separate from the cylinder, into which the steam should be allowed to escape from the cylinder to be condensed there by the application of cold water either outside or as a jet."l Working to this end Watt perfected his patent in 1769. He then proceeded to work out further improvements.

1 Mach, Scientific Lectures, p. 279. Chicago, 1898. 3 Ibid. p. 278.

1 Encyclopedia Britannica, article, " Steam Engine."

How does a scientist work ? These men, one after the other, were seeking the right word to solve a riddle; that is, they were trying to solve a problem which had been handed on to them by men who went before them. Their efforts were not purposeless; they were directed to an end. But how does a scientist work? How did Charles Darwin set about making his marvelous discovery? As naturalist, he accompanied the *Beagle* on its famous voyage from 1831 to 1836. " I have always felt that I owe to the voyage the first real training or education of my mind,"1 he wrote, referring to the riddles he had to solve in puzzling out the geological structure of new and unknown districts. After returning home, in 1837, he wrote: "In July opened first note-book on Transmutation of Species. Had been greatly struck from about the month of previous March on character of South American fossils and species on Galapagos Archipelago. These facts (especially latter) origin of all my views." 2 In his " Autobiography" and his " Naturalists' Voyage around the World " he explains the mental perplexity, which was the origin of all his views, in this fashion: " During the voyage of the *Beagle* I had been deeply impressed by discovering in the Pam- pean formations great fossil animals covered witharmour, like that on existing armadillos...." " This wonderful relationship in the same continent between the dead and the living, will, I do not doubt, hereafter throw more light on the appearance of organic beings on our earth and their disappearance from it, than any other class of facts."

I Life and Letters, p. 61.

2 Poulton, Charles Darwin, p. *id.* New York, 1896.

Now he had his problem. The next step was to find a theory for its solution. In a letter to his cousin in June, 1838, he writes, " It is my prime hobby, and I really think some day I shall be able to do something in that most intricate subject I species and varieties." He gathers facts I " all kinds of facts " I about species and varieties. In October, 1838, he read " Malthus on Population." " Being well prepared to appreciate the struggle for existence which everywhere goes on from long continued observation of the habits of animals and plants, it at once struck me that under these circumstances favorable variations would tend to be preserved, and unfavorable ones to be destroyed. The result of this would be the formation of new species. Here then I had a theory by which to work."

The hypothesis is only the redefining of the problem. First, one must examine the facts that seem to bear upon the problem he started with. That examination tells us that some of these facts bear upon it more intimately than others, and thatits answer seems to lie in their particular direction. They must be interrogated specifically. The hypothesis is the question, or rather the series of questions, which we must put to them. Darwin now had his hypothesis, or theory, by which to work. Then came the years of patient collection of facts in the trying out, both negatively and positively, of the conclusions deduced from the hypothesis. At last the theory seemed to its author to be proved, but he could not trust his own judgment. He must now formulate and publish it, for publishing it or submitting it to the judgment of his fellow workers in the same field is as important as any of the steps of scientific method, since, as Professor Minot has said, " Science consists in the discoveries made by individuals, afterwards confirmed and correlated by others, so that they lose their personal character."1

All are agreed that Darwin possessed that precious human quality which we call "an open mind." But did he simply open his mind and let Nature write her truth upon it ? Would it not be much more correct to say that Darwin had a vastly better quality, namely, an inquiring mind, or a mind that worked? He himself said, "It's dogged that does it," but would " dogged" have done itwithout a question? In other words, is it not the systematic way in which he worked, rather than his persistence, which brought the great result?

1 See Royce, The Problem of Christianity, Vol. II, p. 225. New York,

Discoveries are not made by the aimless accumulation of facts. It is popularly supposed that discoveries are made in another fashion, and that this is neither the way that the great masters work nor the way that the apprentices should take in their preparation. It is Francis Bacon who is chiefly responsible for misleading mankind in regard to this very important matter. Repelled by the scholastic logic, he described the process of discovery as consisting first in the accumulating of facts, and subsequently abstracting their identities and differences, and so deriving laws or general principles from them. " The value of this method," writes Professor Jevons, "might be estimated historically by the fact that it has not been followed by any of the great masters of science." 1 Not the blind accumulation of facts but the putting of questions to nature is the essence of scientific method. The discoverer is the man who is perplexed, who has a problem which has set him to guessing how it may be solved. The problem must be his problem, not a merely abstract one. When it is his problem, it keeps turning itself over in his mind, until he finally hits upon some notion as to how to

1 Jevons, Principles of Science, Vol. II, p. 134. London, 1874.

solve it. Now it has reached the hypothesis stage, it has redefined itself and become a manageably concrete question. This hypothesis may not work. Then he must discard it and find a better one. " I have steadily endeavored to keep my mind free so as to give up any hypothesis however much beloved (and I cannot resist forming one on every subject) as soon as facts are opposed to it," wrote Darwin. *Wherein is the process of finding things out tJte first time different from the process of finding them out tJte second time?* The state of mind which makes discoveries, then, is that which asks questions, which has theories, which anticipates. Learning is not the accumulation of facts, but the purposeful accumulation of facts. Mind is primarily not analytical, but constructive. Analysis or definition is for synthesis and cannot profitably go on by itself. It is motive, purpose, and plan which build the work of the great scientist, as they do the work of the great artist. Liebig, indeed, declared that there was no essential difference between them. Not blind labor but working by a plan gains the end. Now wherein is the process of finding things out the first time different from the process of finding them out the second time ? Human discoveries have not, as a rule, been made by chance; they have been made by the minds which set problems before themselves and laboredpersistently to solve them. It was not by accumulating facts blindly that the steam engine was invented. Is it possible for the student to rediscover it simply by accumulating facts about it? Must he not put himself somewhat in the position of the inventor, ask himself similar questions, supply himself, at least in thought, with similar materials, and construct a result?

Must not the student prefer the search for truth to truth bestowed? The story is told of one of the early philosophers that when a student at one of the great philosophical schools of Athens he asked his teacher to direct him to the problems, saying that he preferred to find the solution for them himself. He was a young Greek Lessing, who preferred to search for truth to having truth bestowed. Were not he and Lessing right ? Has the student, indeed, any choice in the matter? Must he not insist upon undertaking the search for truth for himself, if he is ever to get it? Neither an intellectual, a moral, nor an aesthetic character can be formed otherwise than by a man persistently presenting to himself the objects which belong to it as his good. Passive observation will not make them his. Nature provides him with instructive curiosity and personal needs. Out of that each man must create his own entire body of comprehension and appreciation.

That process should be a systematic one. Merely to tell a person what pictures are good will not make him appreciate them. Neither will telling him why they are good. He must first want to know and himself ponder about them. The reason why the didactic teaching of morals fails, and the didactic teaching of science, history, literature, or any other subject, is because it tries to impart results instead of striving to direct processes.

What is the value of answers which have not been preceded by questions? Mind works by focal- ization. Attention is a name for the fact that experience has a center and a margin. Whatever occupies the center is the object of acutest awareness. Marginal matters shade off into obscurity. Self-protection keeps my affairs, my undertakings, my interests in the center. The rest are negligible, these must ever have the right of way. If I ask a question and you give an answer, I seize upon your answer and try to interpret it in terms of my scheme of meanings. I make it mine. But textbooks and teachers are by no means so thoughtful. They do not wait for us to ask questions they at once begin to supply answers and are not usually polite enough to ask preliminary questions in order to enlist our interest in what they are trying to answer. If attention were different from what it is, if everything that passed beforethe mind produced a uniformly vivid impression, if there were no picking out or focalizing whatever, instruction which supplied answers without questions would perhaps be as good as any other kind. Then Bacon's notion of discovery would be correct. Learning of all sorts would be just the accumulation of facts, for the function of mind would be to mirror nature.

But attention does not work that way. Potential answers to questions may be all about us, but until we ask the questions they will not reveal themselves. We cannot expect to find without seeking, nor to arrive at a destination without first taking precaution to set out for it. The chief difference between the great discoverers and lesser men ,seems to be that the discoverers learned how to put their minds to work, while the others did not. It is the business of education to teach that lesson. It must shift its attention from things to be known and minds which know them to the relations which are to be set up between the experiencing subject and the experienced objects.

If mind is a problem solver what must teachers do? If mind is a problem solver and works by focalization of attention, what does this principle require of teachers? Not to teach blindly, and not to allow their children to study blindly. " Children fear the dark," says Herbart, and by that he meansthat they shrink and withdraw from that which they cannot comprehend and lay hold of. They are naturally eager to learn, but obscurity repels them. They are naturally active, but they cannot act in a given way without some anticipation of what they are to do. Professor Dewey has suggested that perhaps in no other way could so great an improvement be brought about in education as by teachers with one accord seeing to it that children should never set about studying any lesson without first having a clear notion as to just what it is that they are undertaking to learn, and what they are to do in order to learn it. Each single lesson upon a given subject is an organic member of a series. The purposes of the separate lessons must interact to form one scheme of purpose. The teacher who directs the students to the comprehension of the parts must comprehend the purpose of the whole. As a precondition to the reform which Professor Dewey suggests, another reform is necessary. The teacher must know the purpose of each study which he teaches, in order to know how to shape instruction to attain the desired result. Unless education is an irrational proceeding, there must be such a purpose behind the teaching of each subject. The teacher is there to guide the student to socially profitable experiences which will come to him if he will consider this particular body of problems inthe light of certain suggestions as to methods of handling them. He cannot act as a guide unless he knows what it is most profitable for us to see. He must plan the journey before we set out. Is it sufficient if he alone plan the journey?

Must not the student have a general aim in pursuing each study ? Should not the student from the outset know where he is going, or should he be led by faith ? It is customary to say that he is too immature to comprehend the purposes which the different studies serve. He must take them on trust.

His not to reason why,
His but to do and die.

To be sure, he has his questions about their value, and since he is to work at them for some time, he would like to know before he begins what they are for and what the outcome is to be. Those who think it unwise to encourage the doubts of youth would suppress all this and demand unquestioning acceptance which, by a curious metastasis, they call docility. Ought we not to proceed in just the opposite way ? Must not the student know what he is to aim at in order to learn to shoot ? The more definite and purposeful his undertaking can be from the beginning, the greater the energy which it will call forth from him. If his mind is to attend school as well as his body, he must find his own purposesthere. To be sure, he cannot be made aware of the full meaning of the subject before he has studied it. No more can the traveler anticipate in detail what he will see in a strange country before he has set foot in it. Yet, unless he prepares his mind for his journey, the meaning of the objects which his guide bids him look at will escape him, and he will not even see what is there to be seen. The student must have a general aim if his work is not to be merely haphazard. He must face each study he takes up as an opportunity to perfect himself in the particular kind of skill which it represents. Without this general aim he may make the mistake of trying to learn to skate by diligently watching others skate and committing descriptions of how it is done, without once putting on the skates himself.

And must not the student have also a specific aim to make possible the studying of each lesson ? Must he not also have a specific problem to solve in the learning of each lesson ? Theoretically each lesson has a reason of its own. It has been chosen to teach some particular part of the whole process which is to be mastered. To master this phase of the process, it is just as necessary to proceed by a plan as it is in striving to master the subject as a whole. The essence of scientific method, as we have seen, is the location of the problem. Whenit has been found, mind has an end to which to work and can bring its resources to bear upon it. The clearer the anticipation of the end, the more definite the responses which it calls forth. "The nature of the mental life," says Professor Dewey, " may be illustrated as follows: Suppose an individual in a dark room, with which he is wholly unacquainted, and which is lighted up at brief intervals by an electric spark; at the first spark the individual will perceive next to nothing, and that little indistinctly. At the next spark he has, however, this vague basis of expectation upon which to work, and the result is that he apperceives somewhat more. This apperception enables him to form a more perfect anticipation of what is coming, and thus enables him to adjust his mind more perfectly. This process of apperception through anticipation, and reaction of the apperceived content upon the completeness of the anticipation, continues until during some flash he has a pretty definite and perfect idea of the scene before him, although the spark lasts no longer than the first, and there is no more material sensuously present. The sole difference is in the adjusting power of the mind, due to its ability to anticipate.1 As a further illustration of the fact that attention faces the future and works best when preadjusted, hecites the fact that, though the average time which elapses before a sense stimulus, say of light, can be recognized as such is one eighth to one fifth of a second, that if a signal is given before the coming of the sense stimulus, so that the mind can prepare itself, the time may be reduced to one thirteenth of a second.

1 Dewey, Psychology, p. 139. New York, 1896.

Working by the problem is employing the psychology of attention. Working by the problem is nothing more than employing the psychology of attention. But who must have the problem ? It is not enough that the teacher have it and work by it. Each student must have it also. The teacher cannot supply it to them. He can only arouse it within them I it must come out of their past experience. When the teacher states his problem the most that his words can do is to make the learner conscious of a problem already latent in his own mind. It may not be the same as the teacher's. It may, indeed, be of slight worth; but the ability to find out what it is, to postpone one's own problem, and to assist the person whose question it is to find a satisfactory answer for it, is that which makes teaching a fine art.

According to this view the preparation for the study of the lesson is more important than any other phase of study. Every prospective lesson should be resolved into its definite problems beforeanything else is attempted. It is only by acquiring a conscious method of attacking our work that we may really be said to learn anything. The method is applicable to every study and to every lesson. It involves nothing more nor less than for each student to get into the way of asking himself before he attempts to do anything further, " Now just what is it that I am trying to do ?"

"The use of the problem as the form of educating the reason," says Professor Henderson, "... may be said to be the largest outcome of educational reform in the direction of method." 1 There remains much to be done to bring this new-old method into general use. Not the least of the changes it involves concern the textbooks. Most of them have a list of questions at the end of each chapter. The student comes upon them after he has diligently tried to learn the answers of the text, without having had the attention-fixing, force' gathering questions to help him. Should they not come at the beginning, rather than at the end, of the chapter ?

1 Henderson, Principles of Education, p. 273. New York, 1910.

SECTION 9

CHAPTER IX

ORGANIZATION BY SELECTION

The part that the students take in the work of the classroom diminishes progressively as they advance. Why is this? A person who goes from a kindergarten or a primary classroom to the exercises of an eighth grade, a high school, or a college class is pretty certain to note that little children take a much more active part in the work of learning than do the youths and maidens of the advanced classes. The little fellows are full of questions, which neither time nor place can keep them from asking. The older ones can hardly be prevailed upon to ask a question or to express a doubt as to the sufficiency of that which they read or of what has been told them. The disease is progressive. The most unresponsive of all grades of students are college students. To get them to speak out their minds freely upon the subject under discussion is nearly impossible. They prefer to sit clamlike and noncommittal, to receive and not to give. Yet every one of them, when he first came to school, was as eagerly expressive as the children of the kindergarten now are. Something has happened to them as they journeyed from the first grade to the last which has made them spectators and not participants in the game of knowledge. Neither mental habits nor life interests can be successfully cultivated in this passive way. If it is what one does that teaches him, not what one hears, one question raised by a student is more effective than a dozen unasked ones answered by the teacher or the textbook.

Make your schools talking schools. There is no way to make the problem a common possession save by making the school a talking school. As soon as one can be brought to say something upon the subject under discussion, he has committed himself to think about it further. He has defined his own views and become responsible for them to his group. Now he must either support them or renounce them. We may be quite sure that the exercise which he performs just because it is set, without seeing any meaning in it or looking ahead to solve any problem of his own through it, is just " busy work " to him, no matter how old he may be. Merely to be engaged upon a subject matter which, when properly handled, has value is no guaranty that its value is being gotten. Unless the student is searching, we may be sure he is not finding, and what he does when he is not searching, but should be, is deintellectualizing to him. So important, then, is the problem as a means of teaching that it is not easy to make it too prominent. In short it is the problem, and not the answer, for which the teacher is chiefly responsible. Somewhere in his " Autobiography " Herbert Spencer recognizes this by making the sage remark that a good teacher will constantly be raising questions which he will not attempt to answer, but will leave his students to puzzle out entirely for themselves. Such questions as, Does dew fall or rise? What is the difference between walking and running? How does the sap pass from the roots to the branches of a tree ? Wherein was Abraham Lincoln a great man? What is the spirit of our country? What did St. Paul mean when he said " I am a Roman citizen " ? Is it true that the most tragic utterance in Shakespeare is "Othello's occupation's gone "? Why did Socrates insist that he knew nothing?

But the use of the conversation method in teaching has other very great advantages in addition to allowing learning to proceed as problem getting. It permits the student to comprehend the meaning of his own activity from the first and to employ intelligently the methods of discovery and classification. Where it is thoroughgoingly followed, it banishes didacticism altogether.

Education as the learning of definitions. The doctrine of real predicates. Nothing is more astonishing, when we look at it critically, than the curious kind of thing which has at times passed for knowledge and been retailed as such in the schools. The part which the learning of definitions has played and still plays is so great that many teachers seem to hold the view that truth resides in definitions. This doctrine goes back to Aristotle's notion that theoretical knowledge is the contemplation of truth independent of volition. To know anything we must know what it is, not what it does. There are fixed divisions in nature. When we define anything we do not state our own purposes with regard to it. We tell what it *is;* we state its essence. When asked, " What is Socrates ? " we may not say that he is a philosopher, or a marble cutter, or the greatest of the Greeks; we must reply, "He is a man," for that is *the real predicate* to which he belongs. As long as one holds to this theory of real predicates, to know anything is to know to what natural kind it belongs and how it differs from other groups or species which belong to that kind or genus. Learning, then, consists in acquiring *the definitions* of things, for *the definition* explains and unfolds the nature of the thing which it defines.

But take anything I this sheet of paper, for example. What is it? It is something to write upon, a thing to read from, kindling to start the fire with, material to make car wheels out of, stuff to make into pulp from which to manufacture otherkinds of paper, etc., etc. Is it light or heavy, hard or soft, destructible or indestructible ? That depends on what you compare it with. He who would define paper as it is in itself will have a hard task. Which one of the relations into which it enters is *the real* paper ? As an existing thing it is lighter or heavier, larger or smaller, to the right or to the left of everything else in existence. To explain its total significance is impossible. And no one proposition which we can frame in regard to it states its nature any more truly than do a number of other assertions which can equally well be made about it. In short, it has as many definitions as it has properties, and no one of them is to be preferred to another save as it ministers to purpose and leads to valuable results. That is, the business of definition and of classification is not to explain the nature of things, but to set forth their uses.

As long as the doctrine of *real predicates* obtained, strange services were performed in the name of education. Men forgot the form which Aristotle had taught them to follow, but they clung religiously to the notion that truth could be taught only in definitions. Instruction became a very revel of definition-presenting on the part of teachers and definition-acquiring on the part of students. Alcuin, the Saxon teacher, at the court of Charles the Great, does not know his Aristotle well enough todefine by genus and species, but he has inherited the scholastic tradition that truth must be presented in the form of definitions, so he goes about it thus, in one of the dialogues which he wrote for the instruction of young people:

Pepin. What is water ?

Albinus. A supporter of life; a cleanser of filth.

Pepin. What is fire ?

Albinus. Excessive heat; the nurse of growing things; the ripener of crops.

Pepin. What is cold ?

Albinus. The febricity of our members.

Pepin. What is frost ?

Albinus. The persecutor of plants; the destruction of leaves; the bond of the earth; the source of waters.

Pepin. What is snow ?

Albinus. Dry water.

Pepin. What is the winter ?

Albinus. The exile of summer.

Pepin. What is the spring ?

Albinus. The painter of the earth.

Pepin. What is the autumn ?

Albinus. The barn of the year.

The scholasticism of later centuries was so thoroughly convinced as to the finality of Aristotle's doctrine of ultimate differences in nature that it set up an elaborate theory of substantial forms or entities by which to distinguish things. " Fire differs from water," they said, " not only through the position of its parts but through anentity which belongs to it, quite distinct from the materials. When a body changes its condition there is no change in the parts, but one form is supplanted by another." The relations into which things enter and the qualities which they disclose in those relations are their accidents, which are quite different from the bodies to which they attach. To know things now meant to know their substantial forms. The revel of distinguishing, defIning, and classifying, unhindered by considerations of the relations of things, speeded up to a furious rate. To define anything meant to state its essence, not its action. Opium produces sleep because it has a *virtus dormativa*. " The substantial form of fire," said Toletus, " is an active principle by which fire with heat for an instrument produces fire."1 It does not seem possible for a student to increase his knowledge by acquiring definitions such as these.

The doctrine of real predicates to-day. But how do matters stand at present? Is knowledge-getting still conceived to be the learning of definitions ? Professor Mann in his valuable book " The Teaching of Physics " offers the following as illustrations of the method employed to introduce the student to that subject in a text published in 1902:

1 Janet, Introduction to Leibniz' Discourse on Metaphysics. Chicago, 1902.

Physics. Physics is the science which treats of the changes which take place in the physical universe.

The Physical Universe. The physical universe is that part of the universe which is, so far as we know, made up of the two fundamental existences, matter and energy.

Matter. No complete definition of matter is possible. We may learn of the properties of material bodies, but the essential nature of matter is entirely unknown to us. The name is generally understood to mean the indestructible substance of all bodies which are appreciable by our senses.

Energy. The essential nature of energy is likewise unknown. We can measure its quantity, but we know nothing of its descriptive qualities. It may be provisionally defined as the capacity for doing work.

Work. The term *work,* as used in physics, may be defined as the producing of such changes in the relative positions or relative motions of material bodies as would require an effort on our part to produce.

Now how much more does the student know after he has committed these definitions than he knew before ? Just as much as he can supply meanings for out of his own past experience. That is not much, for the list is formidable. This method of study does not articulate closely with life and does not contribute much which the student can use either mentally or physically. Yet everything which is talked about here is in some sense a matter of everyday experience which every reader of the text already knows something about. Is there any reason why learning more about these thingsshould be made so difficult, by abstract definitions, as to be nearly impossible ? Is this cyclopedic system of definitions and theories the best approach to this or any other subject ? Is there not a better way? Professor Mann thinks there is, and this is his illustration of it.

A better way than that of learning definitions. Since mind is a problem solver, if we want it to go to work, we should start with a problem. Here are some which will set every mind to thinking: Is it more work to climb to the third floor up a vertical fire escape or to walk up stairs to the same height ? Why ? Does it require more work to slide a cake of ice up an inclined plane into an ice house than it does to lift it vertically to the same height ? Why? What do you call the lifting, pushing, and pulling which these jobs require ? Can you give other examples of work? Work is a very familiar experience, and to extend its concept is not difficult. The great advantage of this method is that the student has the idea and does the thinking. To go up stairs is work; to climb up the ladder or fire escape is work. Which requires the more work? Almost everyone is ready with an answer, but the immediate answer will not do. For the surest mark of an unscientific mind, as Mrs. Boole has pointed out, is that it does not wait to find out what the truth of a situation which confronts it is, but judges and classifies it right off; while the possessing of a scientific mind is evidenced by the fact that we do not make our judgments instantly, but delay them until we can gather the evidences, apply tests, and study the matter out. It is the suspended judgment and not the judgment which drops instantly upon any subject which should come through training, and here we have a splendid opportunity to present its claims as an ideal of scientific method. Does it require more work to slide ice up an inclined plane into an ice house or to lift it in ? How can we find out the facts and make sure about this? If one wanted to know the exact distance to the wall, he would measure it; and if he wanted to know how much he could lift, he would have to weigh the load. Is it not possible to measure the work done when the ice is pulled into the ice house, and the work done when it is lifted in, and compare them ? To lift a brick one foot requires a certain amount of work, to lift it two feet twice as much, and to lift three bricks two feet requires six times as much. That is, if we multiply the weight by the distance, we shall find the amount of work which has been done in either case and can then compare them.

But a block of ice and an inclined plane up which to slide it into an ice house are not easy to get for our experiment. We cannot wait until ice forms to make it. We want to try out the facts now. How can we? It is for just such a case as this that men have devised laboratories. There is absolutely nothing magical about them—they are handy arrangements for helping one to find out what he wants to know, without waiting for conditions to be favorable outside. In the laboratory we can attach a spring balance to a rope and with it pull a block of wood to the top of an inclined plane, and the balance will weigh the pull of the block. Then we can measure the distance and multiply the weight by the distance. Then we can pull the same block up vertically, multiplying the weight by the distance as before, and compare the two products. The result is a surprise. What shall we say now about the relative work involved in going upstairs or climbing up a vertical ladder ? Have we found out anything about what a machine does ?

Most of the steps of scientific method have been employed in solving this problem. They are very simple and very useful methods of going about our work. The student has learned a little about using them and has a much firmer grip upon the beginnings of science than the repeating of a definition could possibly give him. Now he is in a position to make an attempt at framing his own notion of what work is. Definitions are necessary, but not all definitions. " What is a good definition ?" asks Poincare. " For the philosopher or the scientist it is a definition which applies to all the objects defined, and only those; it is one satisfying the rules of logic. But in teaching, it is not that; a good definition is one understood by the scholars."1 This understanding comes after certain preliminary steps. It must be led up to. It is not an original point of departure.

Shall the student's experience be used in school? Each student brings his own experience to school. Shall it be used there, or shall an abstract body of definitions and textbook principles be made to take its place ? No matter what is done, we may be sure that it is the familiar experience that he will continue to live by. Either the new learning which he is there to get must provide an occasion for the reorganization of his familiar experience and must be grasped by means of it, or it will hardly react or affect him at all. When the classroom is changed into a deliberative assembly for the systematic discussion and testing of the problems which are the crux of all intellectual work, and the teacher presides as the chairman of the discussion, the attitude of the students changes. They collect their own past experiences, they tell them, they draw conclusions from them and try them out, they reword the statements of the textbook, they supply illustrationsof its principles, they furnish percepts to fill its concepts, and they work out homely applications of its lessons and furnish its teaching with the significance of use. In all this, they disclose their own difficulties of comprehension and point their fellows and the teacher to further problems for consideration, which but for their outspokenness would have been neglected.

1 Poincare, The Foundations of Science, p. 430. New York, 1913.

How shall the textbook be used? The textbook, as its name indicates, is a book of texts. Who shall interpret their meaning and make the necessary applications? The answer, I think, must be that the students must do it for themselves; the teacher cannot do it for them. If one attempts to absorb the textbook without interpreting its answers, without indeed first having the questions to which they are answers, without supplementing what it has to offer by what his own experience tells him upon the same subject, and without considering the significance of what he learns in terms of out-of-class doing, is he not subjecting himself to the letter which kills and missing the spirit which gives life ? " Who shall deliver me from the body of this death ?" asks St. Paul. And it seems that he meant this death in life which results from literalism. Is there any way for the student to escape it, save by relying upon the inward man in his learning in the same way that St. Paul did ?

The student must collect materials with which to solve his problems. There is one other emancipation which the student must actively claim. He must not only have his own problems and use his own experience in finding a solution for them. He must learn to consult the experience of other persons than the teacher and other books than the textbook. If his task is simply to learn set lessons, this need not be done, and he will not be taught the wider mastery of the tools of knowledge. Yet as there can hardly be two opinions about the fact that he is in school chiefly to learn how to learn, it follows that he must from the first to the last be taught to use the implements or means of knowledge, and among them books, not textbooks merely, and assuredly not the one textbook with which he is provided. If his lessons are learned only from that, a condition of mental bondage and paralysis of effort will result. The school library and its supplementary books must be used. Even these are not enough. The student must form the habit of finding books for himself at home, in the public library, in other folks' bookcases, anywhere that they can be had, and gathering from them material which bears upon his problems in school. As soon as his learning is approached as a series of problems, his studying gets a new definition. It is now the hunting down of subjects. Instead of a committer of afew paragraphs or pages assigned as a lesson, he undertakes to hunt for all he can find on a given question. He thus becomes a searcher for knowledge ; and by having mental difficulties and defining them as problems, by hunting for facts which are pertinent to them, by organizing these facts together and finding out whether or no they will solve the difficulty, he learns to make his own knowledge I he learns how to learn.

The student must become an active selector of tJte important from the unimportant. There are certain corollaries to this demonstration. The first is that the student must become self-reliant. Passive studying will not make him so. Only by acting on his own initiative can he become a doer. Working by the problem puts him in a position in which he must consciously organize his knowledge by selecting the important from the unimportant, and the true from the false.

Take any lesson I twenty words to be spelled, a column of map questions to be answered, a dozen problems to be solved. Do all the words require the same amount of study? Are the map questions of the same worth? Are the arithmetic problems all equally important ? Take any paragraph or any page of a book. Is each of its sentences of the same value? Book study has a tendency to leave the conviction that they are. Teaching mustcorrect this error. The head of a large office of my acquaintance tells me that he employs as clerks a few graduates of colleges and a good many graduates of high schools; that almost without exception no one of them, when he comes from the school, can take a letter and summarize its contents in a sentence or two; that the ability to seize the main point has not been developed in them. But the ability to take a part of the morning's mail and digest each letter in a sentence or two annotated in pencil upon it is the form of skill which he requires. Another employer of whom I know declares that it is next to impossible to find a secretary who can take a sentence or two of direction and frame a letter to embody it. Yet *precis-writing* and letter construction are not particularly difficult forms of skill, and they are kinds of ability which education of every grade should foster. The habit of finding the main point and distinguishing it from subordinate matter will not come as a by-product of study. Yet every school exercise has a main point and calls for a fixation of attention upon it. The little child in the reading class who does not know what he is reading about, the high-school student who does not know why he is studying this particular lesson and what he is to learn from it, and the college student who tries to put down in his notebook all that the lecturer says, can hardly be said to bedistinguishing values. They are being trained to be " thoughtless thinkers." Only by persistent effort to find the main point and stick to it can that wholesome tendency be established. This natural motive is seldom encouraged in textbooks.

He must separate the true from the false. The student must not only solve his own problems with the assistance of teachers and books, but in doing so he must learn that much that passes for knowledge is not knowledge, and that he is responsible for separating the true from the false. The road to knowledge lies through doubt. The student must become a doubter in order to " prove all things; hold fast that which is good." Descartes begins his " Principles of Philosophy-" with the statement " that in order to seek truth, it is necessary once in the course of our life to doubt, as far as possible, of all things." He resolves to make it a rule of life never to assent to anything which he does not clearly and distinctly perceive. A matter is clear when it " is present and manifest to the mind giving attention to it." It is distinct when it is precise and different from all other objects. It is well known that the senses sometimes deceive us. The dipper handle in the bucket of water seems to be bent. Objects which are far off seem to be near. We do not always hear what is said, and sometimes we seem to hear what is not said. Memory too isa very unsafe guide. Misunderstandings abound. Hearsay testimony is not worth much, though the tendency of the untaught to believe it without.questioning is very great. Men are, many of them, untrustworthy. Much that is printed in papers and in books is not so. Seeing is not believing, hearing is not believing, reading is not believing. Even thinking, if it is not carefully checked up and rendered mistake-proof, may result in error. Mind has a peculiar proneness to delusion. Education does not perform its work unless it makes the learner a keen discriminator between truth and falsehood.

The student must be taught to collect and weigh evidence, to verify statements, to compare authorities, to go to the sources for information in doubtful matters. Where it is possible, he must get into the habit of proving his work. Sufficient unto the day is the exactness thereof, but even little children are able to begin to distinguish truth from falsehood and to pass upon the probability or improbability of the stories they read. Make-believe they love, but they do distinguish it from believe, and upon the continuous fostering of that distinction rests the effectiveness of teaching.

The major ideals of the race are developed by acts of conscious selection called for and persisted in in the work of the everyday studies. To add a column of figures and then to check up one's resultis quite a different operation from summing them once and being satisfied that the answer is correct. To try to get the point of view of the British as well as that of the colonists, or of the South as well as that of the North in the great war, teaches a better lesson than to take the one without the other. The student of geometry should consider carefully what proving a proposition means, for if the process is but an arbitrary series of statements to him, he will learn nothing. The same is true if he stops short of seeing the reason for anything which he is asked to comprehend. Above all, he has a right to be convinced that what passes for truth is founded upon evidence, and he must be encouraged to doubt and to insist upon doubting that which does not convince him. The centuries- old notion that doubt on the part of young people or of adults is sinful must give way to the better doctrine that doubt fosters belief and is its precious precursor.

What should be memorized? While to commit to memory all that one seeks to learn is a bad thing, since it makes comprehension impossible, some part of that which one studies should be memorized. It is a safe rule that nothing should be memorized until it is first comprehended. Most of our learning should remain in that form, but some parts of it must be committed verbally. It is perhaps ascertainly wrong not to memorize what should be memorized as it is to memorize what should only be comprehended, but it is hardly so likely to happen. Memorizing has a place in education, though it is hard to keep it in its place. What would happen if we remembered everything, if the events of yesterday persisted in their completeness ? There would be no to-day. It is only by forgetting the happenings of yesterday that I can give attention to the events of to-day. Forgetting, then, is highly important. Without it there would be no new experiences at all. Yet if it were complete, there would be no new experiences either, for it is through our old experiences that we get our new ones. For the most part, the old ones keep themselves alive. Certain parts of them disappear, but their core remains. Significant experience is rarely completely forgotten. To make it a permanent possession one has only to see to it that its meaning is clearly grasped and a strong wish to retain it developed. Memorizing words is a different matter. Normal forgetting drops the details and retains the significant substance of a matter. Verbal memory strives to retain the detail of language.

The first question to be asked about any matter which should be retained is, Is this something which interest and understanding will keep alive and reasoning restore at will, or are its details so important that it would be valueless if only the substance of it were recalled ? Wherever the letter is indispensable the letter must be remembered, and special efforts will have to be put forth to establish the associations which will fix it in mind. The multiplication table must be recalled not in substance but in exact detail; so must the formula for finding the diameter or the circumference of a circle. Certain grammatical rules and exceptions call for the same treatment. Quotations which get their value not from their thought but from the perfection and significance of its expression must also be recalled literally. Formulas and formularies, poetry and hymns, the basic dates of history, place names and the names of significant personages, are the sort of content which should be committed verbally.1 As a rule, not enough attention is given to fixing them in mind, and far too much to developing a verbal mastery of rational matters which comprehension alone will take care of.

What should become automatic, and how can it be made so ? Certain parts of experience make still heavier demands upon us. All that we strive to learn must be comprehended. Some part of it must be committed to memory and a part must be reduced to habit. *Habit* means " having "; but it is a having which has become organic and nearly automatic. We said a moment ago that the multiplication table should be committed l that is really only a stage in the process of its mastery. The person who, when called upon to multiply seven by nine, has to stop and say over " seven times nine " in order to get their product has only partly learned the combination. The result should come instantly with automatic precision. One does not have to stop to recall the name of a letter nor how to form it when he has need for it in writing. It comes of itself. In shaking hands the right hand presents itself instantly, and in walking, while we may watch where we are stepping, the step comes of itself. Yet all these acts were learned. It is perhaps impossible to indicate in detail just what parts of our learning should become automatic, just as it was impossible to state in detail what parts should be memorized. Examples of what is meant may be given. Working by the problem should become a habit with each student; so should hunting for material to supplement the textbook discussion and volunteering to take part in the class; so should asking questions, stating difficulties, interposing doubts, and insistence upon being convinced. Courtesy should become habitual, and with it the cardinal virtues. A correct bodily carriage and the proper position for work should become organic. The sounding of combinations of letters, the shaping of writing, the spelling of commonly used words, the correct use of speech, and a thousand other details of instruction must become habitual. In forming any habit, it is well to launch one's self with as much momentum as possible. This means that the student must know what he is undertaking and why, and with what expectation he is to go about it. A lively initial interest must drive him forward. It is commonly supposed that repetition will do the rest. This is an error. Repetition, except of a certain kind, is worse than useless. Doing the same thing over and over again commonly results in doing it worse and worse instead of better and better. You and I walk a great deal, and we shall walk a great deal more before we die, but will our walking improve by that practice ? We write a great deal, but shall we write better and better as the days go by because of our much repeating of that act? No, merely doing a thing over and over again does not help us to do it better. There is an old story, which deserves to be taken much to heart, of a boy who persisted in saying, " I have went," until his teacher's patience could bear it no longer. Whereupon he was commanded to stay after school and write the correct form one hundred times. He did so, and in the absence of the teacher at the moment that he had finished, he left this note for her, " Dear Teacher: I have done my lesson and have went home." Repetition without the effort to improve does not make our walking or our writing any better than it was before, and repetition without the effort to improve is of small benefit to any student.

1 See the excellent discussion of this subject in Fitch's Lectures on Teaching, p. 121. E. L. Kellogg & Co., New York.

10

SECTION 10

CHAPTER X
DIAGNOSTIC EDUCATION

An outline history of examinations. When the Emperor Antoninus Pius created the first public professorship at Athens, he unintentionally institutionalized one feature of instruction which has exacted rather a larger tribute of human energy than is its due. For the practice came into being that the teacher who was to be paid out of the imperial treasury should be selected from the whole number of candidates for the post, by means of an examination. And the professors, having learned how important examinations were to themselves, quickly passed them on to their students. Education had gone on for some six hundred years or more in Greece without them, and it had been able to do its work well, as the results of the Socratic age show. Nevertheless they became an essential part of its procedure, and in the eyes of many students and teachers the determining feature in its work.

An apprentice must be able to use the tools of his trade before he can be employed as a journeyman. In medieval days he had to be tried out before he was admitted into the trade gild. The firstuniversities were nothing but gilds or unions of teachers. They adopted the gild method of applying technical tests to the students who sought admission into their company as masters. And examinations grew greatly in importance. Since their trade was to teach, the student apprentice was invested with the insignia and the rights of the teacher only after he had given formal proof of his ability to do the work of the gild. With him " Commencement " was a literal beginning of his life work. It consisted of certain private examinations, a sample lecture or the maintaining of a thesis, and his solemn inception into the gild. This academic ceremony tested the ability of the candidate to do what he was henceforth to do, namely, teach certain books according to certain established methods. It was an ordeal made necessary by its object.

The modern examination has preserved almost every feature of the medieval one save its object. That older one was employed to find out whether a man was fit to do a certain thing that he aspired to do. The modern examination exists primarily to determine whether the student knows what it is conceived that he should know. This change in purpose made it possible for the examination to take the form of written answers to written questions, the first written examinations in Europehaving been given, as it seems, at Cambridge in the year 1702. Written examinations having been invented quickly commended themselves as an easily workable device which every teacher of no matter what subject should apply early and often.

Are examinations trustworthy? No thoughtful teacher can frame the questions, read the students' answers, and endeavor to mark their standing on the basis of one or two examinations without gravely questioning the finality and even the worth of this procedure.

Undoubtedly society must protect itself by demanding that the person who invites its confidence as a practitioner of medicine, law, or teaching shall first be required to submit evidence of the validity of his claims to technical expertness to some competent authority. Such examinations should have no other purpose than to establish the trustworthiness of the person who seeks an opportunity to use his skill in the service of folks who are not in a position, before engaging him, to test it. Their object is to find out whether he can do what he offers himself as being able to do.

But the examinations which are repeated with such frequency in schools are not of this sort. Yet they are often a bar to the future work which the student desires to do. The assumption which is behind the practice of exacting them seems tobe that they are a necessary method of testing the student's fitness and furnish a more reliable gauge of his ability than any other which can be devised.

Are they necessary? The teacher who gives the examination and reads the paper is usually the person who has given the instruction. He has met his classes daily; he can give as many review lessons and exact as much written work from his students as he requires to make him thoroughly familiar with their progress. Why should not his estimate of their fitness be based upon this day-by- day knowledge of them ? " But they must be given a chance to show what they can do in an ordeal." Then the examination is not intended to test their ability, but rather to test their self-control, and it is unfair to them to rate their ability by it. If this is admitted, the defender of formal examinations will most likely take refuge in the statement that the teacher who is not required to hold them at fixed intervals will not, when left to himself, demand sufficient written work to train his pupils in exactness. The examinations are required on this view in order to regulate the teacher, and to mark the students' standing by them is again unfair. Private colleges, as well as school systems, have an undoubted right to attempt thus to supervise the work of teachers both within and beyond their jurisdiction if they want to, but they must rememberthat they make the students pay dearly for the arbitrary uniformity which they thus try to exact.

Are they reliable? The teacher who estimates a student's familiarity with a subject by his ability to answer six or ten examination questions is judging him by means of a sample. He may fail to answer this list of questions, but may pass another list with distinction. In his preparation for the examination he may have worked on the very passages which he is asked to render, or he may have prepared others which have no place in the paper. " But he should be prepared for anything which may come." No, he cannot be prepared for everything which may come, for frequently questions are asked which only a minutely technical interest suggests. Again, the sample performance, by which the student's term's work is valued, may be taken on a day on which he is much below par. There is perhaps as much variation in setting papers as in marking them. If there is, the student has but a slight chance to be adequately judged, for carefully conducted tests have shown a variation of as many as seventy points in the reading of the same papers by members of the same staff of teachers. Uniformity in grading the same papers, even when the teachers of the subject attempt beforehand to agree upon a standard of marking, seems to be quite unattainable. Few school systems and few collegeshave made an effort to standardize their marking. An *A* grade may mean from po to *100* to one instructor, and from p/ to *100* to another; a *B* from *80* to p/ to one and from 70 to ?o to another. One man may mark handwriting, spelling, composition, facts memorized and constructive ability shown, all with the same care; another may disregard everything but the substance of the thought.

Yet the school judges its students, and the students judge each other and, worst of all, themselves by these marks.

They reduce the sciences to features of an examination system. The greatest harm which the examination works is not this gross misjudging of students, but its tendency to reduce the sciences which are taught and the teachers and students who study them to servants of an examination system. Knowledge is not primarily a body of exact answers to exact questions. It cannot profitably be put into the form of a catechism. To emphasize its exami- nable features is to make it arid and jejune. The information test is an appeal to memory. What is committed in order to prepare for it is soon forgotten, and unless the examination is an incident and not the organizing principle in what is done, permanent interests are not developed, the free play of intelligence is not stimulated, and the social utility of learning is obscured. The student studies for theexamination. His scheme of values gets out of perspective. Instead of mastering his subject, he learns to " size up" his teacher in an effort to anticipate the questions which he will probably be asked in the examination, and in place of studying, he adopts the method of " cramming." What is perhaps even worse is that after measuring himself once or twice, he becomes satisfied that he can hope for nothing more than the mark which he has already obtained, and henceforth aims at the degree of efficiency which it represents. Over and over again the students confess, " Oh, I am only a *C* student." The influences that play upon them instead of lifting them above mediocrity confirm them in it. When a mark has once been recorded both the teacher and the student are almost certain to forget that it was arrived at so carelessly that it has but a temporary value. It imposes upon both of them. It is only a most inexact estimate of the student's accomplishment of a particular task, but they take it as an indication of what he can do in a given subject and commonly enlarge it into a registration of his general intelligence.

Realizable reforms. Teachers are much too confirmed in the examination habit to give it up, though a large sized experiment like that of conducting a university or a school system for a term of years without a single formal examination wouldbe of immense service to the cause of learning. The abnormal dislocation of interest which they involve would at least have a chance to right itself; and that would perhaps give an opportunity for the making of a course of study on the basis of reason instead of tradition. But such an overhauling of educational machinery is perhaps out of the question. Yet certain reforms are possible. One of them consists in making the school examination a test of what the student can do, rather than of what he knows. The information test is a memory test. It can be met by " cramming." It is a false incentive to work, and it does not lead to normally organized activity on the part of the student. The doing or capacity test has an altogether different value. It calls for knowledge of what is being learned, not knowledge about it. Questions about isolated facts have no place in such a paper. The student is given a piece of work to perform. He must show his mastery of the facts involved by organizing them to solve his problem. The test is constructive; it is like the demands which life makes. It calls for analysis, but only as a means to construction; thus it organizes knowledge by keeping its parts in place.

The kind of examinations the Chinese now employ. Yet not every problem is a vital problem, and the danger which this kind of an examination runs isof becoming merely a scholastic exercise. The people of China have had rather more experience with examinations than any other body of educators. There is a significant difference in the kind of problems which they now set from those they formerly employed. " In 1828," says Mr. Williams, " the acumen of four thousand eight hundred candidates was exercised during the first day on these themes: Tsang-tsz' said: ' To possess ability, and yet ask of those who do not; to know much, and yet inquire of those who know little; to possess, and yet appear not to possess; to be full, and yet appear empty.' | 'He took hold of things by the two extremes and in his treatment of the people maintained the golden medium.' |' A man from his youth studies eight principles, and when he arrives at manhood, he wishes to reduce them to practice.' | The fourth essay, to be written in pentameters, had for its subject, ' The sound of the oar, and the green of the hills and water.' Among the themes given out in 1843 were these: 'He who is sincere will be intelligent, and the intelligent man will be faithful.' | 'In carrying out benevolence there are no rules.' In 1835 one was, 'He acts as he ought, both to the common people and official men, receives his revenue from Heaven, and by it is protected and highly esteemed.' Among other more practical texts are the following: ' Fire-armsbegan with the use of rockets in the Chan dynasty. In what book do we first meet with the word for *cannon* ? Is the defense of Kaifung fu its first recorded use? Kublai Khan, it is said, obtained cannon of a new kind; from whom did he obtain them? When the Ming Emperors, in the reign of Yungloh, invaded Cochinchina, they obtained a kind of cannon called the weapons of the gods; can you give an account of their origin ?' " 1

Now compare with these the list of questions2 submitted in the year 1903:

Honan. What improvements are to be derived from the study of foreign agriculture, commerce, and postal systems ?

Kianosu and An-huei. What are the chief ideas underlying Austrian and German prosperity ? How do foreigners regulate the press, post office, commerce, railways, banks, bank notes, commercial schools, taxation, and how do they get faithful men ? Where is the Caucasus, and how does Russia rule it ?

Kiang-si. How many sciences, theoretical and practical, are there ? In what order should they be studied ? Explain free trade and protection. What are the military services of the world ? What is the bearing of the Congress of Vienna, the Treaty of Berlin, and the Monroe Doctrine on the Far East ? Wherein lies the naval supremacy of Great Britain ? What is the bearing of the Siberian Railway and Nicaragua Canal on China ?

1 Williams, The Middle Kingdom, Vol. I, p. 552. New York, 1883.

2 Quoted in Brown's " New Forces in Old China " from the Report of the Society for the Diffusion of Christian and General Knowledge among the Chinese, Shanghai, 1903. I am indebted for these very significant references to Mr. D. M. Beers of the class of 1915 of Harvard University.

Shantung. What is Herbert Spencer's philosophy of sociology? Define the relations of land, labor, and capital. State how best to develop the resources of China by mines and railway; how best to modify our civil and criminal laws to regain authority over those now under extraterritoriality privileges ; how best to guard land and sea frontiers from the advance of foreign Powers.

Fukien. Which Western nations have paid most attention to education, and what is the result? State the leading features of the military systems of Great Britain, Germany, Russia, and France. Which are the best colonizers ? How should tea and silk be. properly cultivated ? What is the government, industries, and education of Switzerland, which, though small, is independent of surrounding great powers ?

Kwang-tung (Canton). What should be our best coinage I gold, silver, and copper like other Western countries, or what ? How could the workhouse system be started throughout China ? How fortify Kwang-tung province ? How get funds and professors for the new education ? How promote Chinese international commerce, new industries, and savings banks versus the gambling houses of China ?

Hunan. What is the policy of JapanI.only following other nations, or what ? How choose competent diplomatic men ? Why does China feel its small national debt so heavy, while England and France with far greater debts do not feel it ?

Hupeh. State the educational systems of Sparta and Athens. What are the naval strategic points of Great Britain, and which should be those of China? Which nation has the best system of stamp duty? State briefly the geological ages of the earth and the bronze and iron ages. Trace the origin of Egyptian, Babylonian, and Chinese writings.

Standardizing examinations. But reform our system of examinations as we may, the feeling hasbecome general that even at their best they will not afford sufficient knowledge of what is actually being accomplished by instruction. Educators, as President Lowell has pointed out, are too much given to " relying on formulas." The conviction is fast gaining ground that the claims which are made by them must be submitted to objective measurement. It is necessary that personal opinion should count for less in determining the value of studies, the procedure of instruction, and the worth of the product, and that verifiable methods which any competent observer may employ should be devised to gauge and rectify what is being done. This is so large a program that several generations will be required to carry it out. In fact, there is no end to such an undertaking. What it really means is that those who follow the calling of the teacher must set themselves resolutely to get a more exact knowledge of what they are doing than educators have had hitherto.

Quantitative exactness comes from counting. Mathematics is not more certain than logic, but where logic must answer with a bare Yes or No, mathematics can tell how much. Whatever can be reduced to a common denominator can be counted, and whatever can be counted can be compared, and this comparing of group with group, condition with condition, discloses principles which may be appliedto produce the results which are desired. Counting offers the very great advantage of enabling one to become acquainted with the significance of facts without being overwhelmed by direct contact with them. By fixing attention upon aggregates, empirical laws are discovered which the study of individual cases would not reveal. Besides, the study of aggregates enables us to supplement and verify the hypotheses of deductive reasoning.

In view of these very great advantages, it is not strange that a social science such as education, with limited opportunities for experimental research, should call to its aid the resources of statistical investigation.

Measuring some of the results of instruction. The application of statistical methods is indeed not new in education, for studies of cost and attendance have long been made. What is proposed and attempted now is a much more thoroughgoing distribution of these figures and the numerical coordination of many more facts. It is possible to measure cost per student hour of instruction, and in that way prevent disproportionate expenditure. It is possible to measure the efficiency of a school system in terms of the success and failure of its students to meet the requirements of the different grades, and it is possible to measure the effectiveness of a school system in terms of its power toattract and hold its students after the compulsory attendance law has set them free to decide whether or no they shall continue in its classes.

Is it possible to measure the quality of the product ? The examination fails to do that. Its questions are not weighted, the same credit usually being given for correct answers to each of them. There is no objective standard of accomplishment. The markers vary greatly in the value which they put upon the papers. Is there any way by which standards can be established and degrees of approximation to them distinguished and counted ?

It was not possible to know the amount of land that one man sold to another, or the distance from one place to another, until a unit of linear measure had been adopted. It was not possible to determine the amount of oil or wine a man sold to his neighbor until a standard of liquid measure had been devised. And it was not possible to fix the value of commodities which were offered for exchange until a unit of exchange value was established. Just so the discovery of the principle of specific gravity and the invention of the thermometer made possible exactness of distinctions which had been vague and uncertain before.

If the results of instruction are to be determined with exactness, they must be measured, and before they can be measured, scales must be devised withwhich to measure them. A great deal of energy has already gone into the effort to make such scales. Professor Thorndike was the first to attempt to develop one for measuring handwriting. The unit of his scale equals approximately one tenth of the difference between the best and the worst of the formal writings of one thousand children in grades five to eight. The differences represent equal fractions of merit, as determined by the judgments of from twenty-three to fifty-five competent judges, who graded the samples of writing into groups according to their estimate of general merit. This scale, then, is as much more exact than a single individual's judgment of the degrees of excellence in writing as the judgment of fifty-five competent judges of general merit in handwriting is more reliable than the judgment of one. But what is general merit in handwriting? Is it an arbitrary pronouncement of the persons who act as judges, or is it itself measured by a principle ? The chief requirement in a standard measure is that men will adopt it. For them to adopt it, it must commend itself to them. Dr. Leonard P. Ayres thought it better to measure handwriting by legibility than by general merit, since legibility can itself be evaluated in terms of the differences in time required to read the several grades of handwriting ; and by means of elaborate experiments, heconstructed a scale for measuring legibility. It must be noted that this scale measures only that one aspect of writing. It does not enable us to determine what slant should be used, for though it shows that the most legible writing is the vertical slant, instruction in the use of that slant has been abandoned in the schools for other reasons. Speed, which is an essential element in handwriting, is not measured by this scale.

Hillegas developed a scale for measuring the degrees of merit in English composition. Ballou has endeavored to perfect it. Buckingham has sought a measure of spelling ability. Hanus has devised a scale for measuring work in the translation of Latin. Elliott has endeavored to provide a measure of teaching capacity. But the most elaborate effort of all which have yet been made in this direction is Courtis's series of tests in arithmetic.

Mr. Courtis says that " educational measurements are sharply differentiated from ordinary examinations in many ways. The purpose of examinations is to measure the efficiency of individuals; that of educational measurements, to determine the efficiency of the teaching process itself. Examinations are varied from grade to grade and from topic to topic, but if the results from standard tests are to have meaning, exactly the same tests must be given under rigidly uniform conditions to all I whethermen, women, or children, and without regard to their ages, grades, or types. Under uniform conditions the men, women, or children may be measured with respect to any single mental ability covered by a test just as truly as they may be measured in respect to any single physical trait, as length by the use of a single standard unit. We do not hesitate to measure both the new baby and his grandfather with the same foot rule, or to weigh them both on the same scales. Further, an examination once used can seldom be repeated. But results from repeated trials of a mental test may have the same general significance, from the point of view of growth, that repeated measurements of the weight of an individual may have. In educational measurements, repeated tests not only may, but must be, made." 1

What these scales do and do not tell. While the ideal of scientific or exact measurement is greatly to be commended, there is grave danger that the weighing and measuring apparatus may not be as scientifically correct as they should be, and that they may be used in ways for which they were not intended. The yardstick will not tell you whether or no you ought to buy carpet, but if your room needs it, it will help you to determine the quantity which you require. The scale will not tell you how many pounds you ought to weigh, but only how much you do weigh. The foot rule will not tell you how large a house you should build, but it will help you to make an intelligible plan. Moralists are in the habit of distinguishing the criterion from the standard. The criterion is an " ideal"; the standard is a measure. Whether it is well for a man to own his own home or not is one question. How large the lot is which he has bought is another. The first one cannot be answered by counting or measuring. The second one can. " Science," says Mr. Balfour, "depends on measurement, and things not measurable are therefore excluded or tend to be excluded from its attention." But life and beauty and happiness are not measurable. " If there could be a unit of happiness, politics might begin to be scientific."1 Certain results of instruction can be measured, as, for example, the degree of legibility of handwriting, when matched with the corresponding sample on the Ayres scale; or accuracy and speed in adding or subtracting numbers when tried by the Courtis test. These standards help us to know a great deal more exactly than we can know without their aid the value of the results which we are getting I in terms of the standard. But there are very important features of the learning process which they do not measure and do not attempt to measure. One of these is the interest which students take in the process which they are acquiring; another is the value which they are learning to attach to it; a third is the obstacles which they are overcoming; and a fourth, the degree of momentum with which they are likely to carry these processes on after leaving school. One trouble with the examination as a test of learning was that it got results only on the day of the examination. If results only are measured, will not processes be neglected ? The main object of education is not to mature results, but to develop processes in such a way that the growth of after years will perfect them. It is not the business of the elementary school to impart that degree of skill in calculation, in penmanship, and in the use of language, which only the maturer years and the specialized training of the higher commercial schools render possible. If the work of the elementary school is tested by standards which may be used to measure its work as well as the finished work of professionals, will not the inevitable result be to foster a professionalizing of its product ?

1 Proceedings of the Harvard Teachers' Association, 1913, p. 32.

1 Quoted by Sir Oliver Lodge, *Science,* September 19, 1913.

Another kind of scale which we need. Sit down with a package of forty specimens of children's handwriting in front of the Ayres scale for measuring penmanship. What will it tell you about them ? It will help you to find out what each specimen is worth, as you compare it with the scale, in terms of handwriting. That, precisely, is never a problem which the working teacher has to solve. His question is essentially different. It always takes the form, What is this bit of writing worth, as coming from a ten-year-old or a twelve-year- old child ? An abstract measuring of handwriting or arithmetic is one thing. It requires a positive standard. But the measuring of a given child's performance must be in terms of the child as well as in terms of the subject matter. For this purpose we need a relative scale. One might as well attempt to measure the manhood or womanhood of little children as to measure any other developing quality which they possess in terms of a positive standard.

The scales thus far worked out enable us to distinguish degrees in arithmetic, writing, composition, etc. They also measure deficiency from an absolute standard. They not only tell us how much we have, but they tell us how much we ought to have I how much we fall short of perfection. That is, they are both standard measures and standards of performance. But the carpenter's foot rule does not tell him how high to build the building; he must consult his plans for that. The balance will not tell you how much you should weigh, but only how much you do weigh. These two concepts must be kept apart. The standard measure ofinstruction should be a device by which to measure the stages of instruction, not a statement of an ideal to be attained in it. Why can we not have scales which establish the norms of attainment and the degrees of variation from them of children in the first, second, third, fourth, fifth, sixth, seventh, and eighth grades? The scales which we have do not measure increments of growth; they measure deficiency from an absolute standard. When the Ayres handwriting scale is tacked up on the wall of a schoolroom, the children bring their exercises and compare them with the one in the upper right-hand corner, for that they think stands for perfection. And frequently the teachers think so too. A scale which would show the normal results in penmanship for children of their age, with the subnormal and the supernormal arranged by degrees above and below it, would not be so discouraging and would enable both the teacher and the pupils to measure their work. " We do not hesitate to measure both the new baby and his grandfather with the same foot rule, or to weigh them both on the same scales." Quite true, but to say that a child is fifty inches high and weighs seventy-seven pounds is not to know anything scientifically about him. Such facts are only the " substratum of everyday judgments " upon which scientific measurements and coordinations are based. How old is he, and howdo his present height and weight compare with the norms of height and weight which have been established, or are being established for children of his age ? The scientific physician weighs and measures him in pounds and inches that he may weigh and measure him in norms. That is, he weighs and measures him quantitatively that he may weigh and measure him qualitatively. Why does he want to compare his condition with norms of growth ? Not that he may record an interesting fact in the child's natural history, but that he may, if possible, find out what there is to be done to better control and direct his future. That is, his weighing and measuring of the child is for diagnostic purposes.

Right here we come upon three very helpful considerations. The first is that science employs and coordinates two kinds of measurement to get such results as educators are trying to get by one. The second is that the process of establishing norms is different from the process of measuring actual conditions. And the third is that these actual conditions, when coordinated with the norms of development, serve only to direct a search for matters which must be adjusted to bring about the results which are desired; that is, they furnish an aid to diagnosis.

The scales which have been devised seem to confuse the criterion and the standard. They attemptto measure quality and quantity on one and the same yardstick. This is due to their borrowing the nomenclature of the percentage system of designations1 of merit from the scheme of marking examination papers, and applying it in a way in which it is never employed in that system. On the Ayres writing scale *go* means the most legible sample of writing which was submitted, but a teacher of writing frequently marks a third-grade paper po, meaning by that only that the work conforms to her conception of what third-grade work near its best should be, and in so far as her conception is correct, she is right. If the scales are intended to measure quantitative differences only, their distinctions should be designated by neutral symbols which leave no implication that they furnish a standard of what is to be done. The samples in the right-hand columns might be called x degree writing, those in the next one y degree, and so on. Thus the scale would be a standard measure of recognizable degrees of difference in writing and would run no risk of being mistaken for an exemplification of the kind of writing that children should be doing. If a given child's exercise, when measured by the standard, is found to be v degreewriting, the teacher's next step is the same as that of the physician, when told that the child weighs 50 pounds, namely, to find out what the age of that child is, and then to compare that result with the norms which have been established for children of that age. In scientific knowledge the fact is conceived " in relation to the facts by which it is surrounded." It is one thing to distinguish degrees of perfection in handwriting or arithmetic, and quite another thing to put the proper value upon a given child's accomplishment in handwriting or arithmetic. The standards which we have judge arithmetic, but not the child-learning-arithmetic.

1 This criticism does not apply to Thorndike's scale for measuring handwriting, which has a distinct advantage over some of the others in this respect.

Norms of growth cannot be established by statistics alone. How shall we establish in the several subjects the norms of growth with which it is necessary to coordinate the positive results attained in order to measure the relative efficiency of the child ? Statistics alone will not furnish them to the educator any more than they will to the physician. Statistics furnish facts | the norm is a realizable ideal. The normal health of a given locality may be very different from the average or mean condition of health of its people, as the norm of healthfulness which Colonel Gorgas followed in cleaning up the city of Havana was very different from the average of the conditions as he found them. The norm is a model, something to work toward, an availableoptimum, an ideal which is attainable when the causal connections are properly controlled, and not merely a registration of the effects of conditions as they now are. Just as it is the function of every development in the science of medicine to contribute its quota to the ever-growing conception of what health may be, so it is the function of every genuine discovery in the field of education to play its part in shaping the realizable norms of instruction. The science is a practical one, and every method of discovery which yields results must be employed to inform us concerning its possibilities. What is being done may conceivably fall far short of what should be done, in which case a statistical study of it will not be of great directive value. Up to 1870, reading was almost everywhere taught by the alphabet method. The most thoroughgoing tabulation of what was being accomplished by that practice would not of itself have established the normal way to teach reading. Advance in every line comes by studying its defects intensively rather than by establishing a consensus.

Psychology, child study, medicine, and the logical criticism of concepts which belongs to the principles of education must evaluate the results which the statistical and experimental study of education furnish. Only by such a coordination is a science of education possible.

Grave danger that statistical methods may be applied where they do not belong. There is grave danger that statistical results may assume to furnish the ideals of education and determine courses of study just as systems of accounting have attempted to organize the administration of cities. One might as well attempt to make a school system with a pickax as by the results established by a system of accounting only. The mariner's compass does not tell you where to sail, but only where you are. You must consult your charts, the winds, the weather, and the seaworthiness of your craft, to find out whether you are in danger, and your destination and your log to find out how to port your helm. The statistical study of results tells what has been done; but other considerations, among them the nature of the undertaking and the nature of the child, must be combined with it to determine what should be done.

An illustration of this tendency. A specific illustration of a possible misdirection of educational effort through the power of the tests which are imposed is the following from the Annual Report of the Superintendent of Schools of New York City for 1913: "As every school man knows, examinations largely determine the character of teaching. What the examiner calls for, that the teacher will teach. Now, the Courtis tests in arithmetic constituted an examination, and this examination I fear may lead, in the minds of inexperienced teachers, to a wrong conception of their aims. These tests laid unusual stress on *speed* in the manipulation of numbers.

" We all know that speed in the manipulation of numbers is an important intellectual asset in the business world, and that it is well worth a serious effort to attain. I submit, however, that accuracy is much more important. What will it profit a business man to have his clerk add up a column of figures in thirty seconds if the resulting sum is incorrect? The commercial and manufacturing world demand accuracy as the first qualification in figures, and accuracy should be our first aim in teaching arithmetic.

" Now the Courtis tests lead in precisely the opposite direction. In that examination the children were driven at top speed throughout. They were allowed no time for checking or verification of results. If our teachers should follow the example set in that examination, they would do an irreparable injury to our pupils.

" Some years ago I advised our principals and teachers that in their practice work in addition, children should be required to verify the result for each line of figures before proceeding to the next line. The method suggested was to add each line first up and then down, and as often as necessary until a uniform result was obtained. I advised similar precautions in the other fundamental rules. I still cling to this theory

I not speed at the expense of accuracy, as in the Courtis tests; but accuracy first and speed afterward should be the aim of the New York schools.

" Some such notion seems to have occurred to Mr. Courtis since the New York tests were given, as he writes me that he has since somewhat modified them."

The power to test is the power to control. The nature of the test shapes the work which is given and the scheme of values which is set up. This new device is a two-edged sword in education. It must be handled with care. The very effort to measure results instead of processes seems to shift the focal point unwarrantably.

A truer measure of results. Those who devised the tests have no such intention. We can measure process only in terms of results. What they desire, doubtless, is a means of checking up processes. But the burden of our whole discussion has been to show that education is to be measured by its success in setting up vital processes in such a way that they will be indispensable to the person who has once learned to use them as long as he may live. According to this view, the true test of the efficiency of a school is not to be found in anexamination, no matter how carefully devised, which would determine whether an eighth-grade student can read, write, add figures, spell the words he should spell, pass in history, or what not. The true test of the school's efficiency consists in finding out whether or not that student, thirty years after graduation, say, is still a man who reads, who'writes and spells well, who uses scientific methods, who is historically minded and still in particular, not in general, shows that in his youth he began to learn a way of life. It seems next to impossible to devise and apply a system of tests of this kind. Yet these are the features of education which determine its worth, and until we can gather the measurable results of this great experiment for a number of years we shall still be in the land of vagueness and uncertainty. In charity work it has become customary to follow up the case that has been helped, through a term of years. The good home follows its sons and daughters, taking account of their successes and failures through life. In these days of eugenic inquiries, extending back over a number of generations, a scientifically devised examination of its students, by a school, after they have had thirty years in which to deepen or forget what they learned in it, does not seem unworthy of repeated trial. The results of all other examinations would speedily sink into insignificance beside this.

The proper way to use rules and standards. But there is another kind of examination with which education is beginning to concern itself in a very lively fashion. It is the systematic effort to fit his work to the student, not the student to the work. The principles which science formulates are shorthand expression of facts, each of them " a type of a series of possible facts."[1] The well-founded distrust of uniformity of procedure as based upon such generalizations, rules, or laws, can be met only by remembering their nature and learning how to use them. It is the misuse of the standard, not the standard, which must be fought. No general principle can embrace all particulars. We have a system of courts to fit the laws to particular cases; a body of practicing physicians to fit the principles of medicine to the conditions of their patients. It is not by establishing uniformities that education will become a science, but by establishing uniformities in connection with the particulars out of which they grow, and to minister to which is the sole reason for their existence.

It is said that no two engines made from the same pattern consume the same amount of fuel, develop the same power, require the same amount of lubricating oil, disclose the same structural weaknesses, nor last in service for the same number ofdays. An engineer who attempted to treat them in exactly the same way would destroy, in part, at least, the usefulness of one of them. This principle of dissimilarity is deep seated in nature. It impressed the philosopher Leibniz so profoundly that he regarded it as a fundamental fact in the make-up of the universe, pointing out that no two leaves on the same tree are alike, and no two beings have exactly the same nature. Some folks believe that there is only one right way to do a thing, and all the other ways are wrong. Mr. Kipling did not agree with them when he wrote:

1 Enriques, Problems of Science, p. 81. Chicago, 1914.

There are nine and sixty ways of constructing tribal lays
And every single one of them is right.

It is altogether likely that there is no one uniform and eternally right way of doing anything, that the right which is not merely an abstraction is always a function of a situation which is individual, and will never repeat all its details in any other situation.

The true place of uniformity in education. But while situations are different in details, and individuals and even machines are different, and call for differences in treatment, situations are also like other situations, and individuals like other individuals, and machines like other machines. There are uniformities in them all, and if we take these uniformities as part of what we are dealing with,not the whole, we shall find them useful. The United States Government finds it useful to uniform its soldiers, but if it attempted to put a uniform amount of cloth into each soldier's dress, the result would be unhappy. It applies the principle of uniformity where it belongs and finds it serviceable. Just so in education, school systems ought not to be alike, or to expect to be alike, in the details of their administration, their courses of study, their methods of teaching, or the objective results which they get. The principles of education must be applied, which means that they must be interpreted in terms of the situation. Within the system the same application to individual conditions must be made, or life-killing regimentation will usurp the place of education. Those schools therefore are the best which are doing their utmost for the individual child. Since it is vastly more important to have a mentally alive child in a schoolroom than a dead subject of study, we must not make the mistake of defining education in terms of a fixed quantum of knowledge or even of rigidly prescribed studies to be pursued. What we seek primarily is to help each child to use his own mind. To get and keep a living and expanding interest, a searching, reflecting, organizing, using, mental activity, going on in young children, it will be necessary to meet them where they live. Instruction must adapt itself tothe interests of the place in which it is given, to the traditions and culture of the homes from which the children come, to their age and advancement, and to their mental variations. Uniform courses of study, uniform textbooks, uniform methods of teaching, and uniform results must go the way of outworn shibboleths. Their uniformities must vary to meet individual cases.

Clinical psychology and education. The very practical science of clinical psychology has for its object the studying and diagnosing of individual mental behavior, in order to find out how to minister to its needs. This science has not developed so far as to lead the men engaged in it to regard themselves as the servants of a body of theoretical distinctions which are of value in themselves. They are keenly practical in what they are doing, and the classifications which they make are diagnostic merely. Professor Wallin distinguishes two general classes of cases I those in which the mental variations are primary and the physical disabilities accessory, and those in which physical deviations are primary and mental variations sequential. Under the first class he groups *feeble-minded children,* insisting that the bettering of their condition is essentially an educational problem; *retardates,* of whom he believes there are not less than 6,000,000 in the schools of the United States, some of whom are retardedsimply because the curriculum is abnormal, others because of arrested development, others because their environment handicaps them, and others because of physical defects; the *supernormals,* who need only special opportunities for work, but without them develop a kind of enforced mediocrity; *speech defectives* such as stutterers, lispers, etc.; and *incipient psychotics,* or children who show the beginnings of mental disorders. The second class is made up of cases of malnutrition, rickets, tuberculosis, heart trouble, chorea, etc. Here the treatment called for is primarily medical; in the first class it is primarily educational.1

Here is a tremendous engine of discovery, whose significance to parents, children, and teachers is beyond estimation. It provides a knowledge not of groups or of attainments in studies, but of the individuals to be educated. For the hit-or-miss methods of a more or less arbitrary objective procedure, this practice would substitute a basic principle of organization, the diagnosis of the child himself. When we measure in order to determine regulative principles, we must in the last resort measure the primary reality with which we haveto deal. That primary reality in education is the individual child. Courses of study we may change, for the demands of society are conventions which can be made or unmade, but the nature of the individual child is given. Everything else must be related to it.

1 Wallin, "Clinical Psychology," *Science,* June 13, 1913. See also the *Psychological Clinic,* edited by Professor Witmer; *The Training School,* published by the New Jersey Training School, Vineland, New Jersey; and the publications of the Psychopathic Institute of Chicago ; particularly Dr. Healy's recent book, " The Individual Delinquent."

Guidance based upon diagnosis. Another application of diagnosis to education is the important activity known as vocational guidance. Its function is to help young people to find the callings for which they are fit. To help them in this way demands an elaborate study of the distinctive requirements of the several occupations, and a careful investigation of the traits and capacities of the given individual who seeks advice as to what occupation his talents indicate he should follow. The problems which this procedure present are so very difficult that only a beginning has been made in solving them. That there are individual traits that should serve as indexes of the specific functioning which a young person can reasonably hope to perform, no one perhaps will deny; but what these distinguishing traits are remains to be found out. A number of men and women are at work upon this problem. Much has already been done to collect and distribute information as to the requirements which a number of occupations make. The literature of vocational guidance is already largeand is growing rapidly. There is need for a similar fitting of studies to mental aptitudes while education is going on.

The most significant statement which I find in Mr. Courtis's reports of the vast and important work which he has performed is this: " My thesis is that we must practice what we preach; the teaching of children is a far more complex task than even the wisest of our leaders have realized; that we must begin over again and evolve new methods, new courses of study, new ideals of education generally, and that all must be based upon the central idea of determining and ministering adequately to individual needs. At present, our school products are uniform from city to city, because a certain degree of development is easily secured by any method; because, also, even a very great increase in time and effort produces only slightly greater results. That is, the benefit of class instruction is limited, and the limits are quickly reached. Improvement can come only by the adoption of methods and opportunities for supplementing class instruction with work with individuals." 1

A thoroughgoing reconstruction of class teaching. By far the most thoroughgoing reconstruction of class teaching of which I know has been going on since the beginning of the year 1912 in the StateNormal School located in San Francisco. Dr. Frederic Burk, the president of the school, has recently issued a bulletin setting forth an outline of their plan and results, under the title " Lock-step Schooling and a Remedy." The considerations which led them to abandon the class system of instruction were: first, admitted failure of that system to produce creditable results; and second, the fact that from one third to one half the pupils remaining in the schools in a large number of typical cities are above the age which is normal for their grades. This condition seems to be common to schools, no matter how well they are administered or taught. Accordingly, the cause must be some common feature which lies behind teaching and administration. They began to suspect the class system as the enemy of the child for the reason that though children are different, the class system required them to take a lesson of the same length each day and to learn it with the same degree of thoroughness. It assumes the same degree of simultaneous attention in all, in spite of illnesses, absences, worries, and all kinds of personal ups and downs. It assumes that all will progress and be promoted at the same rate. It measures a pupil's work not in terms of his own ability, but by comparing it with that of a fictitious average pupil who has no flesh-and- blood existence but is merely a dividing line to

1 Proceedings of the Harvard Teachers' Association, 1913, p. 44.

separate those who are above the average from those below it. The class system does permanent violence to all the pupils; for those who could travel faster than the average are shackled to it, and those who should go more slowly must seem to keep up with it. This required keeping of the step robs both kinds of pupils of natural inducement to work and prevents the normal growth of individuality. It makes the brighter pupils dawdle and the slower ones it discourages. Indeed, it does much more harm than this, for it perverts instruction. For, take two children who are set to learn the same lesson I let it be the combination of eight plus five; assume that one boy learns it and the other does not. What should the next lesson be for each ? It should be different, but under class teaching it is not.

The prime fact is the pupil. He is different from his fellows in motives, speed of comprehension, difficulties, and firmness of grip. But it is he, and not the nonexistent "average pupil," whom the schools must put in the way of becoming a self- reliant pupil-thinker. How to get every student to put all his talents at interest is the problem.

The faculty of the normal school resolved to cut away obstructions. The first one which it met was the textbook. Its language is incomprehensible, hence its words are memorized. It provides lessons of the same length for pupils who require lessons ofdifferent lengths. Current texts are made up for the most part of facts and definitions to be memorized. They contain no adequate provision for reviews. " Knowledge," the faculty said, " does not consist in learning definitions, nor in committing statements about facts. It consists in using them." They set out to teach each student to write a sentence and to use the multiplication table, rather than to define a sentence without being able to write it, or to recite the multiplication table without being able to multiply numbers correctly. For this purpose flexible texts1 had to be produced, providing many varied exercises on the same principle for the student who required much familiarity with it to make it stick, and few for the pupil who mastered it quickly, and supplying a wide range of work from which a selection could be made to fit the needs of each.

The makers of these lessons sought to omit all abstract explanations from them, to make each lesson begin as the learning of a doing set forth in it so simply that each pupil can master the problem by his own effort. Difficulties are introduced one at a time. There are duplicate exercises in plenty, making the lesson sufficiently long to develop accuracy where it is slow in growing, or to allow a few trials only and a quick advance to thenext lesson to the person who masters the principle at once. Reviews are automatically provided by being embodied in subsequent lessons.

1 Such texts suitable for individual work have been published by Ginn and Company under the title " Minimum Essentials."

The results. " We are astonished at our immediate results, in changed spirit, in reawakened young ambitions and energy, in rapidity of pupils' progress, and in our own enthusiasm," writes Dr. Burk. The individual classroom is a workshop where each student is busy with his own work. It is the function of the teacher to learn what each one can do and the motives which prompt his doing. She is there to help him to his work, and to give him the encouragement of approval and assistance when he needs it. Going from desk to desk to help pupils who perhaps did not need it, these teachers soon found to be debilitating to their scholars, for " substantial learning " can be secured only by the pupil " putting his own mind through the given process." The familiar recitation is completely abandoned, but when, by individual doing of work, a group of pupils have familiarized themselves with an epoch of history, a geographical area, some problem of industry, or other unit of study in a given field, the classroom becomes a forum in which they are brought together for a " Socratic discussion," for the mutual clarifying of their ideas upon it. Such deliberations have a regular place in the weekly program.

An effort is now being made to work out a course of study to cover eight years, the allotment of work in each year to be determined by what the slowest pupils can reasonably accomplish in that time. Since each one advances as rapidly as he can, the others will complete the work in a shorter period. No one is demoted, or turned back to repeat a grade. Promotion by a card is a merely nominal recognition of what has been accomplished. The school day is divided into short work periods, and each child's work is regulated in such a way as to vary his activities according to his need. Home study is entirely abolished. From twenty-five to thirty per cent of the pupils are advancing much more rapidly than the usual class rate. From ten to twenty per cent are going more slowly than under the class system, but they are doing thorough work, and not giving an appearance of keeping up only.

This plan differs from earlier forms of individual instruction in that it abolishes the individual recitation of a memorized lesson. A teacher guides the work of as many pupils as under the class system. The correction of written work is the real difficulty. But the pupils do that, for " the principle is sound that, as a means of learning in most subjects, there is no exercise quite so productive and thorough as the correction of errors."

11

SECTION 11

CHAPTER XI
LEARNING TO WORK WITH CONCEPTS

The essential thing in education. As long as schools exist the most important thing about them will be not their budget, nor their buildings, nor their administration, nor their teachers, nor their examinations, nor even the branches of learning which make up their course of study; the most important thing about them will be what their students do. These other things are necessary that the work of schools may go on, but they are only means to that end, that end, their work, being a doing on the part of their students, a doing of such a kind that the students will have to go on repeating it as long as they live, a doing therefore which the experimenting of the ages has found to be necessary and which their fellow men in days to come will require from them. But these other things I the money needed for the maintenance of the schools, the buildings needed to house them, the corporation or the board of education, the president of the college, the master or superintendent of schools, the professors or the teachers who " give the instruction," and, most of all, perhaps, the subjectswhich they study I keep getting in the way of the students' work and arrogating to themselves by turns a kind of monopoly of attention which keeps the nature of the educational undertaking sadly obscured. However, experienced teachers of teachers are not at all uncertain as to the relative importance of these elements in the educational process. When they send their apprentices to visit the workshops of other teachers they charge them above everything to watch what the students are doing, and after that to give attention to what the teacher is doing to facilitate the students' work. When they inspect schools themselves they keep their eyes upon that aspect of them. For what the learner does is the essential thing.

What should the student do? To find out what the learner should do one must hunt down the meaning of a good many very familiar words | words whose meaning their very familiarity has tended to confuse and obscure. Concerning them one must ask himself the Socratic questions: What is education ? What is knowledge ? What is mind ? What is truth ? What is science ? What is literature ? What is culture ? What is a vocation ? What is personality? etc. In short, he must criticize the concepts of education. The human endeavor which goes at matters in that way is called philosophy. It forces one to trace the connections and relations of things which the sciences take for granted and study separately. One who studies chemistry is not required to study the philosophy of chemistry, and one who studies physics or biology may neglect to criticize the assumptions of these sciences, but one who studies education must not neglect to work out his own philosophy of education in the light of what men have already thought about its meaning and its purposes, for education is an integrating process, and to make wholes or personalities it must proceed from the knowledge of the whole. All real philosophy has education for its object, and all real education must ground itself in philosophy.

A superseded theory of education. There was a theory of mind which maintained that human experience was built up by impressions. David Hume was its prophet. "An impression first strikes upon the senses and makes us perceive heat or cold, thirst or hunger, pleasure or pain, of some kind or other. Of this impression there is a copy taken by the mind which remains after the impression ceases; and this we call an idea. . . . To give a child an idea of scarlet or orange, of sweet or bitter, I present the objects, or in other words convey to him these impressions; but proceed not so absurdly, as to endeavor to produce the impressions by exciting the ideas.. . . This priority of the impressions is an equal proof that our impressions are the cause of our ideas, not our ideas of our impressions." 1 These isolated or separate impressions associate themselves into complexes by a sort of spontaneous generation, and mind Hume describes as a "bundle or collection " of these single impressions " in a perpetual flux of movement." Though he begins with the impressions and expressly disclaims any implication as to their source, he constantly implies that they are, as in the case of scarlet or orange, presented by objects.

We have here, therefore, the basis of a simple and generally accepted theory of education. Impressions and ideas, which are their copies, come to us from objects. To give the learner the impressions the teacher must present the objects. If they are only presented, the impressions will come of themselves and the ideas, or copies, will remain. Spontaneous, or natural, association will do the rest . The whole process of education is synthetic, a building up of single impressions one after another within the mind, and a trusting to their spontaneous fusion to organize them.

The theory which has superseded it. This psychological doctrine reigned with nearly undisputed authority until Professor James published his " Principles of Psychology" in 1890. Even Immanuel Kant, who gave Hume the credit of having roused-him from his dogmatic slumber, accepted Hume's notion that experience starts with a manifold of impressions, clear cut, distinct, and separate, though he proceeded to show that mind does not allow them to bundle themselves as they please, but organizes them according to certain principles of its own nature. Experience getting was for him still a synthetic process, a putting together of bits or units of experience into the mosaics into which mind, because of its organizing nature, insisted upon building it.

1 Hume, A Treatise of Human Nature, Bk. I, sections I and II.

But Professor James announced a radically different view, and knowledge getting took on a correspondingly different definition. The most obvious thing about consciousness, he said, is that it is a stream. We start not with separate and distinct impressions. We start with a confusion, with a vague, onrushing, unbroken flux of feeling. We see nothing clearly at first, we hear nothing clearly, we feel nothing clearly. Experience is not built up out of separate impressions at all. Education is not a building up of such impressions by the presenting of things to deposit them and their copies in the mind. " Out of this aboriginal sensible muchness attention carves out objects, which conception then names and identifies forever I in the sky ' constellations,' on the earth 'beach,' "sea,"cliff,' 'bushes,' ' grass.' Out of time we cut ' days' and ' nights,"summers' and 'winters.' We say *what* each part of the sensible continuum is, and all these abstracted *whats* are concepts. *The intellectual life of man consists almost wholly in his substitution of a conceptual order for the perceptual order in which his experience originally comes"* 1

This doctrine reverses the problem of education. According to Hume and his successors its task was that of presenting impressions. According to James its task is that of carving out objects from the continuum of feeling. The teacher is no longer a com- pounder of impressions I his duty is not to objects, but to what goes on inside the mind of the learner.

How does this carving out of objects proceed? We bring with us certain instinctive, selective tendencies which force the aboriginal flux of feeling into consolidations or clusters which we call things. But very strangely, as we have seen, we do not name these separate or isolated things. Our naming is all of classes or kinds of things. If we would name a thing as it is experienced at a given moment, we must employ a phrase such as " this table," " the book there," or " that horse." Our names are all class symbols or devices for dealing with recurring experiences of similar kinds. They indicate past experiences and expectations as well as the present particulars to which we apply them.

1 James, Some Problems of Philosophy, p. 50. New York, 1911.

It used to be thought that these general names or concepts grew out of particulars or percepts; that one must have had a certain number of experiences of *men* before he could by abstraction arrive at the notion of *man.* But psychologists now teach us that the concept and the percept arise together. " The child begins with what seems to be a' general.' His earliest experiences, carried over into memory, become general copies which stand as assimilation nets for every new event or object. All men are 'papa,' all colors are 'wed,' all food 'mik.' ... It is only partially true that the concept arises from the percept at all. It is rather true that the two arise together, by the same mental movement, which is apperception or motor synthesis. Going back again to that neglected period, infancy, we may ask, as a matter of fact, what takes place.

" Suppose, after the very common method of the day, a single presentation, A, in the infant consciousness ; then suppose it removed. The child is now ready to germinate forward and backward, future-ward and past-ward. He remembers and he expects. Viewed as *memory,* his experience, A, is particular, a sensation, after a time a percept. But it includes more than his simple receptive state. He reacts to it, and so stands ready to react to it again. This readiness is his *expectation,* | the tendency he has to a definite reaction; and as the onlyone it stands ready to 'go off' on any kind of stimulus which is locally near enough to discharge that way. His memory has become *scJiematic* of the future viewed as expectation, it is the whole of the child's reality; it is what will happen, for it is all that can happen; he knows nothing else. Whatever then actually does happen is at first reacted to as A, and remains A, by this active confirmation, if it is possible for the child's consciousness to keep it A."1 Thus mind by its own inherent nature selects what is vital to its necessities from the sensory continuum, and from it constructs its world. It organizes its surroundings in accordance with its own constitution just as the tree or the plant does. From concepts of the first degree it proceeds to concepts of the second degree, and in due order to concepts of the third degree, by progressive consolidation distinguishing new particulars within the sensory flux and operating with them as anticipations, differentiating and classifying as long as consciousness continues in this state of existence. For it is not only the baby's immediate sensory life, but every man's at every age, which is a big, blooming, buzzing confusion from which his mind must select its own materials of objects and processes according to his vital needs. The instrument with which hemakes this ever-continuing selection is his reaction system, his system of concepts, his body of ways of anticipating and sorting the sensory flow. The problem of education then, like the problem of philosophy, concerns the nature and use of concepts. They are the vessels with which the water of life may be dipped from the stream of consciousness and applied to human uses.

1 Baldwin, Mental Development, Methods, and Processes, pp. 309-310. New York, 1906.

The nature and uses of concepts. The thinker, says Plato, is one who is able to distinguish the one from the many and to recognize the one in its various combinations with actions and things. The knowledge which he seeks is knowledge of the one, is knowledge of the nature of things. These are hard sayings and have been persistently misunderstood. The one of which Plato is speaking is the circle as distinct from circles, the triangle as distinct from triangles, the truth as distinct from truths, justice as distinct from particular acts of justice, goodness as distinct from this, that, and the other good deed. The thinker is one who is able to discern the circle or the triangle in the shaped things he must work with, and thereby determine their character and the uses which he can make of them, or who, having the pattern of truth or justice in his soul, can and will shape his deeds and the whole ordering of his affairs accordingly. And knowledge is of the one because he who wouldknow and work with circles must know the circle; he who would serve truth must know what truth is; he who would establish justice on earth or his corner of earth must know what justice is; and he who would grow plants must have a concept of plant life to organize his deeds. The words which we use always express more than the facts which they seem to designate. When we talk of a point, or line, or circle we are talking about things which we cannot draw or visibly represent. When we speak of the truth, or of equality, justice, humanity, plant life, etc., we speak of existences which eye hath not seen nor ear heard, but which it has entered into the mind of man to conceive. They are not things, but thoughts which order and arrange things; they are ideals by which we organize the perceptual stuff of existence. The concept is the way we relate the parts of experience, the principle or law, the meaning or significance of the things with which we work. The things with which we work pass away, they flow by us, they are in ceaseless change, but their meanings do not change. This round column will in time be broken up, the lie which was told a moment ago will be forgotten, the acts of barbarity which that nation committed will be blotted out from the book of human remembrance, but how long will circles be circles ? How long will truth be truth ? Howlong will justice be justice? Here are life interests which do not pass away.

The relation of concepts to things. Let us illustrate the relation of concepts to percepts in a figure. Let the lines *A B* and *C D* represent the ladder of life, or the course through which one

D

passes from birth to death. At every moment in that course he is surrounded by an infinity of particular things, some very few of which his necessities force him to take note of and to use. One after another, as occasion arises for them, he picks them out from the vague which surrounds him

and names his anticipations of them. This group is bread, that is clothing, that is shelter. This body of related facts is geometry, that is religion; this is morals, that is knowledge. The vertical lines which cross the moments of existence are our life interests or ways of organizing the incessant flow of particulars. They are our concepts, or principles by which we thread our way through this maze. Since they are our life interests and the interests of the race, they have a much greater permanence and import than the quickly vanishing facts or particulars which stream by so ceaselessly. Yet while they are vastly more important than the facts of any single moment, we must remember that their sole function is to harness this flux of things, that their only value is that they bring facts to us and take us to the facts or experiences which we desire.

The kind of knowledge which we seek. We conceptualize only a small part of our experience. We might, as we have seen, name and classify the many appearances and reappearances of the table, the chairs, the books, and of every other object which we see, hear, smell, touch, or taste, at every possible distance and from every possible point of relation, just as we might classify the books in our libraries by the number of times the letter *a* or the word *the* or any other letter, word, mark, or discernible difference appears in each. But we donot, and the reason why we do not is that the conceptualizing of such percepts would be of no possible use to us. What we seek is a reality which will help us in our work, not a reality which we can only describe. The notion that knowledge is the description of reality takes no account of human purposes, and leaves us rudderless victims of a horizonless sea of facts. While it is true that concepts are not the sensible equivalents of sensations, they are the changes which we bring about in percepts to organize them into activities. History may be described as a faithful account of what happened in time past. The history of the Civil War then would be a full report of the events of the war. But these events were infinite in number. They not only cannot be found out and described, but most of them would be of no significance even if they could be. The first thing which the historian must do is to select from this mass of happenings that very small part which had significance. He schematizes these into a systematic whole and offers us this as the history of the period. Dead facts he endeavors to omit, but living facts, that is, events and considerations which the bulk of folks to whom he addresses himself must still take account of and reckon with, he seeks to incorporate into his story. Because the facts which are pertinent to the vital interests of one generation are not always those which were pertinent to the interests of the generation which preceded it, each generation must rewrite the history of the past from its own standpoint. The sensory experiences which the men of the past had and the records which they made of them have not of course changed, but our interest in these events has changed. So through the nets of contemporary interest we strain the ancient happenings over and over again, and the result of this straining we call history. Each new generation thinks that it has at last succeeded in writing the definitive account of antiquity, but the next generation is as unwilling to accept its interpretation as final as it was the interpretation of the men who went before it.

This same process of selection and interpretation determines the content of science. The known facts do not change, but the questions which we put to them are kaleidoscopic in their variety. Even geometry, which was long held to be the perfect specimen of absolute knowledge, has recently undergone surprising development. There was a time when men looked upon " an eye for an eye " and " the divine right of kings " as unchanging principles of social knowledge. We look upon them now as almost inexplicably self-imposed limitations of human intelligence. In this way the final truths of past generations are outgrown.

Knowledge cannot be given. It comes only from searching. Since knowledge seems to insist upon being not what we find but what we take, not what is given but what is hewn out of an infinity of possibilities, what goes on inside the mind of the learner is more important than what was in the mind of the textbook maker when he wrote his textbook or of the teacher who explains it. Since they cannot communicate their thoughts any more than they can communicate their toothaches or their headaches, they must help their students to find ways to generate similar thoughts within themselves. They must give up the effort to present knowledge ready-made and content themselves with the humbler, but much more exciting, task of surrounding their disciples with inducements and necessities to make it, each out of his own experience. A school conducted on this principle is in the active, not the passive voice. Its students are engaged in asking their own questions and in defining their own purposes. So far as they can they carry out their own plans; they bring up from their own observation and past experience whatever they already know that has a bearing upon the problem whose solution they are seeking; they question folks both inside and outside of school to get the information that their specific undertaking requires them to get; they consult books and libraries. Inall this they are learning to work by purposes, to put two and two together to accomplish what they want, to hunt in many ways for what is needed but is not at hand, to pick out that which has much import from that which has little import, to make up their own minds as to the value of the materials and statements which they find, to frame their own projects, to use their own language, to doubt, to question, and to prove.

Such a school is a workshop as certainly as a manual-training room or a foundry is. In it one learns to work with mental tools and acquires skill in using his own mind. The tools which he learns to use are concepts, and the materials which he learns to work up by their aid (just as he learns to shape lumber with the plane and saw to the plans of boxes and boats which he has formed) are his own sensations, percepts, and thoughts.

The best description of tJte process of education which I have found. Strangely enough the best description of the process of education which I have found is in one of the books which have begun to circulate widely since the war. It is the work of a Frenchman, M. Georges Bourdon, and is devoted to setting forth the views of certain representative Germans whom M. Bourdon interviewed concerning their own country, its ideals and plans of development, both within the limits of Germanyand in relation to their neighbors. This book was published in France before the war began. Among the representative Germans whom M. Bourdon interviewed was the principal of an elementary school at Neukolln near Berlin, Herr Samuleit, whose statement of the aims of instruction is as follows: " It is, indeed, customary in all our primary schools that the lessons should consist nearly entirely of conversations between master and pupils. We make of instruction an exchange of ideas, and avoid wearying and saturating minds that are still fresh and untrained. We consider it as a kind of heresy to teach for hours with pupils ranged before us who listen but do not speak. All the efforts of our actual system are, on the contrary, directed to awakening the pupils' interest and mental energy during the class. We wish, as we say, to replace as much as possible the ' study school' *(Lernschule)* by the 'working school' *(Arbeitsckule),* that is to say, a school in which the pupil, through personal experience, instructs himself. I mean that we desire to substitute for the passive absorption of the master's teaching, the active research of the pupil. We would have the former gradually disappear in favor of the latter." 1 If such a conception of teaching as this had obtained in the gymnasiums anduniversities as well as in certain elementary schools of Germany, the present " over-drilled " condition of the German mind with its awful consequences could hardly have been.

1 Bourdon, The German Enigma, p. 263. London, J. M. Dent & Sons Ltd., 1914.

What learning to work with concepts means. Learning to work with concepts is a very different process from that which goes on in many schools of elementary, secondary, and college grade. One does not sit quietly and pore over books or listen to lectures or recite what has been committed. He does not approach knowledge timidly as a thing let down from above, which exists in itself and for its own sake and whose parts were eternally perfected before he came here. To him it is not like that prevailing German notion of the state, a thing apart from and above the individual men and women who compose it. To such an ejective idolatry he is not under bondage, for it is not fostered within him. He learns from the first that knowledge is man- made; that its purpose is not to describe what is, but to help folks in doing what they want to do; that since it is an instrument the only way to master it is to use it; that every subject which we study is an enumeration of certain important human facts, the attitudes which men have learned to take toward them, the processes by which men have learned to handle them, thus far, most successfully, and an invitation to the student to go and dolikewise with them. The states of which we read are ways of living together, from which we have to choose that one which most appeals to us and in our thoughts and acts to give it being. The truth of which we are told is a process of searching out meanings which we must learn to employ; the logic which we study is a series of safeguards which each of us must learn to observe; the ethics which we discuss has for its object the bringing of each one of us to select his own point of view and method of thinking and acting in order to embody them in conduct; the literature which we read is a series of runes which have charmed the race and some of which will charm us if we but pick them out carefully and let them say themselves over and over again in our souls.

The origin of the idolatry of knowledge.   Every educational discussion before Aristotle was on some aspect or other of the question, What shall a man do in order to live well ?1 Every educational discussionsince Aristotle has more or less consciously implied the query, What subjects shall a man study in order to be educated ?1 The great classifier had no intention to substitute names for acts, but ever since he compartmented the field of human endeavor subjects of study have tended to appear as ends in themselves rather than as means to action. When my boy comes home from school and is asked what he studied to-day, he replies that he studied history or geography. But when I ask what history or what geography he studied, he is at a loss for an answer. Indeed, the question seems to him to be irreverent. Like him, most young learners and a good many old ones personify and attribute real

1 Isocrates, like his master Socrates and his fellow student Plato, thought of education as learning to do what man must learn to do in this world, not as learning to know. He states his position in these words:

" Whom, then, do I call educated, since I refuse this name to those who have learned only certain trades, or certain sciences, or have had only certain faculties developed ? First, those who manage well the daily affairs of life as they arise, and whose judgment is accurate and rarely errs when aiming at the expedient. Then, those who associate in dignified and honorable fashion with all with whom they come in contact, bearing easily and good-naturedly what is unpleasant or offensive in others, and softening, as much as possible, their own asperities of manner. Further, those

who never become the slaves of pleasure, and who by misfortunes are not unduly cast downlbearing themselves in their presence manfully and in a manner worthy of our common nature. Fourthly, and most important of all, those who are uncorrupted by good fortune and do not lose their heads and become arrogant, but, retaining control of themselves as intelligent beings, rejoice not less in the goods they have acquired at their birth by their own nature and intelligence than in the benefits that have been cast in their way by chance. Those whose souls are in permanent and harmonious accord, not with one of these things, but with all of them, these, I say, are wise and perfect

men, possessed of all the virtues. This is my opinion with regard to educated men."
I Isocrates, Panath. 30, ff. (Walden's translation in " The Universities of Ancient Greece ")

1 It was Aristotle's division of knowledge into theoretical and practical, and his description of theoretical knowledge as due to contemplation independent of volition and as existing to enable us to know and only to know, that supplanted the sounder teaching of Socrates and Plato and introduced confusion into the world. This ancient error must be corrected and the sounder view of Socrates and Plato must be accepted once more, or education shall never have an organizing principle.

existence to the subjects which they study, and then perform ritualistic ceremonies before the idols which they have reared. Some worship philosophy and long to serve her; others venerate literature and would spend their lives in adoring her; others objectify science and talk of her as a goddess; others speak of the study of Greek as though healing could be had by the touching of these garments. This is the false use of concepts. That mystical element must be dispelled from studies ere they can serve us or we each other by means of them. We must get on speaking terms with them, we must make them articulate with everyday affairs. The question is not what philosophy or literature will make out of me, but what I can make out of philosophy or literature. Knowledge does not consist of committing the labels which have been attached to things and trusting to their magical virtues to produce effects. Man's proneness to attribute independent efficacy to the creations of his own hands is indeed a dangerous phase of the human tendency to delusion. Sciences, literatures, conventions, and institutions when they have once been shaped exact a tribute of respect quite out of keeping with their nature and their origin. We treat them as things; they are collections of uses, meanings, practices I verbs, not nouns. No amount of veneration for, or nominalisticfamiliarity with, the several branches of knowledge which we have hypostatized will persuade them to impart their grace. The folks who invented them intended them to be ways of acting I means but not ends in themselves.

A renaming of the sciences is needed. They are noun substantives, they should be nouns participial. Reading, writing, spelling, numbering, drawing, forging, weaving, cooking, painting, when we study them, have an immense advantage over physics, chemistry, mathematics, history, logic, ethics, and literature, just because their names end in *-ing,* leaving no doubt as to their nature and the kind of service which they undertake to perform for us. The other studies do not invite us to take them by the hand. Their *-ic* and *-ry* endings intimate to us that they are not of our world and that their perfection has long since been accomplished. Every child finds the alphabet and printed books here when he comes; his duty is to use them, and the process is called reading. He finds numerous songs and musical instruments; the acts to which they invite him are singing or playing or listening. The word *music* is a name for the songs which the race has sung and the instruments which it has formed for its playing. It also connotes the singing or playing or listening which each newcomer to the planet is invited to take part in; that is, it is the name of aprocess as well as of an achieved thing. When we hear the word *music* we are more apt to think of singing and playing or listening than we are of the ready-made historic contribution which has to be rendered or interpreted. The *-ic* of this word is really an *-ing.* It signifies something to be done, an activity to be undertaken. But the connotation of *ethics, logic, history, literature, mathematics, biology, geography, chemistry, physics, rhetoric,* stresses the ready-made-thing aspect of these studies and leaves their functional purpose quite obscure. If our view of them is correct, their prime value does not lie on their factual side, but in their directive uses. They are not things, they are socially profitable ways of acting, and when we study them our primary purpose must be to learn to use their processes. If they are present-day activities rather than historically fashioned objects, we should think of them accordingly, and, to assist ourselves in doing so, should employ words ending in *-ing* to indicate their meaning and their value to us. Instead of referring to ethics, we would talk about the study of doing or behaving; logic would be most commonly spoken of as the study of thinking or reasoning; history would be searching, substantiating, or constructing the outline of the past; literature, appreciating or criticizing ; mathematics might be mathematizing; biology, thinking about life; geography, the imaging of theearth; chemistry, compounding; physics, moving; rhetoric, persuading; composition, composing, etc.

The advantage of such a facing about in language would be an immediate and nearly universal clarification of thought, which would very shortly effect radical changes in educational practice. The most significant change of all, perhaps, would be in the attitude of the students. Instead of being confused and uncertain, as they now are, as to why they are invited to pursue certain studies or how they are to study them and what they are to try to get out of them, their way would be reasonably clear before them. Just as no child is ever very uncertain as to what he is expected to do in the activities which we call reading and writing, so they would not be uncertain as to the part which they are to take and the results for which they are to strive in each subject which they study.

Learning according to this view is always specific. It is always an effort on the part of the learner to himself acquire skill in handling socially profitable material in socially profitable ways. The skill which he acquires, the habits which he forms, the reactions which he learns to make, are always keyed off or called forth by situations recognizably similar to those in connection with which they were acquired. Some of these situations are rare; some are nearly universal. When one form of efficiencyenters as an element into the handling of a great variety of situations, the only caution necessary to make it available in all of them is to see that the context in which it is developed is sufficiently wide to make it consciously connectible with all of them. As the purpose of developing the reaction in school is that it may not only be used in school but throughout life, it is necessary that school practice should be built up about life situations, that school learning, in so far as it can, should take the life form. This principle limits mere exercise work, and offers a test by which profitable studies and parts of studies can be distinguished from those which are merely conventional and profitless.

Nothing can be clearer, it seems to us, than that the purpose of education is to develop certain specific attitudes, expectations, reactions, ways of going to work or comporting himself in the varied situations of life, on the part of the student. What we seek in all that we do with him is a certain self- initiated doing on his own part. He is an apprentice who comes to us to learn the elements of certain highly valuable and humanly indispensable trades. These trades all have to do with the shaping of human experience. Their content has resulted from the accumulated efforts of men in past days. It is a series of standpoints, attitudes, rememberings, methods of reckoning, ways of attacking, etc. whichhave been found to minister to human purposes. When the apprentice comes he is initiated into them in the hope that they will produce in him similar feelings and that, having seen their significance, he will learn to employ them in shaping the affairs of his own life. His apprenticeship is spent in learning to control human experiences by means of concepts. A typical subject matter is given him just as the alphabet is given him, and he is required to learn to work by means of it. Every study which he pursues is not only a body of results of which he must become mindful but a system of processes which he must learn to employ for himself as long as he lives; for the subject matter of the study in connection with which he learns them is only a typical sample of the subject matter of life. When he studies economics, or history, or literature, or any other subject, he is learning how to use their regulative concepts in ordering his own goings and comings, both mental and physical. If this is so, the results which he produces and should be expected to produce must not be measured by an altogether objective standard; they must be taken in terms of his own capacity, past opportunity, present health, encouragement, distractions, etc. The one vital question at all stages of his progress will be not Does he conform to our preconceived notions of uniform results to be attained as determined byexaminations, grades, standards, scales, etc.? but Does he use his own mind in the degree that he can in mastering the processes upon which he is engaged ?

Concepts must not be misused. One final word of warning is necessary. If intelligence works with concepts and education has for its task the teaching of men to work with concepts, the legitimate use of concepts must be distinguished from the illegitimate. The uniformities which we construct are devices to assist us in interpreting experience, guides to tell us what to watch out for, not final statements of what we are certain to find in every case to which we apply them. The doctor who diagnoses a case and decides that it is pneumonia treats it accordingly, but watches to find out whether the reactions which follow confirm his diagnosis, and revises his judgment accordingly. His application of the concept is tentative and ministerial. A child of ten who delights in setting grass afire is labeled a pyromaniac. The men and women in charge of him when he is twelve continue to refer to him as a pyromaniac, at twenty or forty he may still be referred to as a pyromaniac, and his chance to reestablish himself as a trustworthy individual may by this classification be denied him entirely. Likewise, an institution child may be robbed of his birthright of equalopportunity because his teacher has decided that all institution children are failures. A first-grade child who has been taught to read by one system and is then transferred to a school where a different system is in use may be so helpless in the face of his new difficulties as to be named and treated as a dullard, to his irreparable loss. The student who does not produce the fixed results in a given form or subject may indeed be able to produce highly creditable results under other conditions. If he is classified finally on the basis of the symptoms which he exhibits at any given time, great wrong will be done him. The concept is always a summary of experience up to date, it may not fit the facts of to-morrow; its function is to lead or guide. It does not claim to furnish an infallible statement of what will happen. To use it as though it were more than tentative is to misuse it.

12

SECTION 12

55

Dewey, John, on the "supreme

art,6 204

Diagnostic education, 282-322 ; ex-

aminations, 282293; measuring

renults of instruction, 2941312;

true place of uniformity, 312-314;

clinical psychology, 314-316; vo-

cational guidance, 316-317 ; re-

construction of class teaching,

3 i7-3"

TJoctrine of general discipline, 59-

103. .$v a/K General discipline

Doctrine of real predicates, 260-266

Doing, learning for, 170-171; the

end sought, 171-174; ways of,

in music and athletics, 174-175;

knowing from, 175-179 ; the

teacher's attitude toward, 179-

184; verbal study and, 181-183;

relation of each study to, 183-

184 ; education and, 190-193 ; cul-